D1562144

Now Bring Your Joy To This Wedding

Couples In Premarital Preparation

Norma S. Wood

and

Lisa M. Leber

CSS Publishing Company, Inc., Lima, Ohio

Copyright © 2002 by
CSS Publishing Company, Inc.
Lima, Ohio

Scripture quotations marked (NRSV) are from the *New Revised Standard Version of the Bible*, copyright 1989 by the Division of Christian Education of the National Council of the Churches of Christ in the USA. Used by permission.

Library of Congress Cataloging-in-Publication Data

Wood, Norma Schweitzer.
    Now bring your joy to this wedding : couples in premarital preparation / Norma Schweitzer Wood and Lisa M. Leber.
        p.   cm.
    ISBN 0-7880-1881-7 (alk. paper)
    1. Marriage—Religious aspects—Lutheran Church. I. Leber, Lisa M. II. Title.
BX8074.M3 W66 2001
248.8'44—dc21   2001037935
                                                                                            CIP

For more information about CSS Publishing Company resources, visit our website at www.csspub.com.

ISBN 0-7880-1881-7   PRINTED IN U.S.A.

With thanks for the life and teaching
of
Herbert W. Stroup, Jr.

Table Of Contents

Preface

Congratulations! You are reading this because you and your spouse-to-be have made the joyful and awesome decision to get married. There's a lot to be done, of course. Whether you are planning a large wedding or a small one, an intimate family gathering or a service to which your whole neighborhood is invited, you probably are already getting a sense of the almost overwhelming amount of preparation that needs to be done.

This book is designed to help you in some of that preparation — but it's not about picking flowers or seating arrangements or honeymoon planning. It's about exploring the special nature of marriage as a commitment lived out by two distinct and unique individuals, who have histories and personalities and wants and dreams, and who come together in and through their promises of faithfulness in a very special way to build a life.

It's about helping you to "bring your joy to this wedding."

You'll get more of a sense of purpose and methodology of this book as you read Chapter 1, the introduction. But there are a couple of things we want to say here which will help you understand why this book was written.

The church is very realistic about marriage. Marriage involves human beings who are imperfect and who live in an imperfect world, and so marriage and family will be experienced as both a gift *and* a burden to those who enter into it. This book helps the church live out its call to nurture and support couples as they prepare for all the different kinds of dynamics, events, and learnings that are the reality of marriage.

The church also views marriage as a vocation, as a special place in which the Christian partners are called to live out their baptisms — to glorify God and to love their neighbors. The church doesn't understand marriage to be just "a private romance" between two spouses, but a relationship which has a communal dimension for learning how to be faithful in love. Marriage as vocation, then, is something a couple grows into, and the church is called to assist that growth into marriage in all its phases.

Although growth into marriage is a life-long process, the church has rightly recognized the wedding as the start of a new and significant life passage. Thus it has widely urged its clergy and congregations to offer premarital counseling and ministry to couples who are preparing for marriage.

This is an important and challenging task. And in this book, which is addressed to the couple in pre-marital preparation, you will find tools to do some of the sometimes hard work of:

- understanding how the family cultures each of you brings to the marriage influence the process of becoming a married couple;
- examining the implications of the marriage covenant and offering you helpful tools and perspectives as you make and carry out promises of love and faithfulness; and
- integrating your understandings of God and the faith community into your own developing relationship.

We hope, too, that as you work through this book with your pastor or priest, you will develop a foundation for any post-wedding pastoral care from him or her.

With that in mind, we invite you into the next pages.

Chapter 1
Introduction

Many people decide to marry, even in the face of some tough odds. Statistics tell us that for every two weddings there is a divorce, and yet ... men and women just like you continue to make a commitment to each other through marriage. What makes marriage so compelling? What draws people to this union of husband and wife? Why do people want to commit — *publicly* — to a life-long relationship? And why is the church involved and interested in marriage? In supporting your marriage relationship? The answers to these questions have something to do with Christians' belief that marriage is a gift from God. Whether we are really conscious of it or not, when a man and a woman promise lifelong faithfulness to each other, something of the Holy is made known to us humans. In marriage, God offers human beings the chance to participate in something sacred. In marriage, we are given a glimpse of God and the love God revealed to us in Jesus Christ.

It's awesome that a man and a woman, led by God to make a commitment to one another, promise to face the years together, to experience jointly the future's joys and sorrows!

But marriage is even more than that. Marriage highlights the good news that God has created human beings to enjoy the gift of relationship, the gift of community. God's desire for us is that we experience life together: God created us male and female, built up families and communities and tribes and nations, gave us commandments to help us live in loving relationships with one another. Ever since Adam and Eve, life together has been the mark of God's people.

God knows that life is too hard to be lived alone. Humans need each other to survive. We cannot be all we are meant to be without each other's nurture and support, without touch and love and forgiveness, without security and safe places to draw the strength to live in a broken and harsh world. In God's graceful love, we are given the yearning to be with one another, to live in relationships that are holy and sacred. A marriage is one of those relationships — one in which two people are drawn uniquely together. At its best, a marriage is a place of trust, intimacy, a place where a man and a woman know each other as no one else does, where they learn to sacrifice and compromise, forgive and love with all their being.

The failure rate of marriages and the hundreds of "self-help" books about relationships remind us that all of this is hard work. As much as we idealize our spouses-to-be, as much as we long to have a marriage of mutual love and support, understanding, and togetherness, men and women preparing to make their wedding vows recognize that such relationships do not just "happen" — they are the result of reflection, conversation, and God's grace.

This workbook is intended to get the process of reflective thought and conversation going for you as you prepare for your marriage. We began the introduction to this book with the good news that God is at work in love. The God who became flesh for us in Jesus Christ, who made love known in the real, live person of the Son, continues to make that love known.

One of the ways God loves us is through the people God sends into our lives, people like our spouses. We experience love and forgiveness, compassion and mercy through our spouses, as well as through the community of people surrounding us. These people of God also nurture our growth and development. As we live life in partnership with one another, we learn the art of compromise, we develop conflict resolution skills, we are given unique opportunities to experience things in life we might otherwise not have experienced.

The danger in talk like this is that we can view the relationships in our lives, like our marriage, as being only about our personal satisfaction and self-fulfillment. Marriages sometimes can be seen only in terms of our happiness, and perhaps the happiness of our spouse and children.

Marriage And Community

But marriage is not just about you. It is not just about you and your spouse, either. Marriages have everything to do with the larger community, with the whole Body of Christ, the whole people of God. Marriage is a relationship where we are empowered to live out our baptism, where we are nurtured for our mission to be disciples of Christ. Before we are husbands or wives, before we are parents or children, brothers or sisters, friends or coworkers, we are baptized children of

God. Before anything else, we are chosen by God to be God's very own — and in that act, chosen by God to abide in God's great love with one another.

In *Whisper from the Woods*, a beautiful children's book, Victoria Wirth uses the story and pictures of the life cycle of a forest to talk about life and death. Acorns fall from trees, seedlings root in the forest floor, trees grow, storms ravage the woods. One of the most powerful pictures in the book is a picture of the forest where you can see the tree roots underneath the soil. In the earth, you see that the roots all are drawn as if they have hands growing at the ends of them. The roots are all woven together in the dirt, intertwined, reaching out to one another, hand grasping hand. The narration of this picture speaks of the interconnectedness of the roots of the trees, which enables each tree to stand firmly and grow, blossoming and bearing fruit.

That's how it is for us in the Body of Christ. In our community of the children of God, we are all connected. Our lives are woven together by God, intertwined in the soil of Christ's love; we reach out in that love to grasp one another so that we can stand, growing and bearing fruit together.

Each of us is essential to this community. We need each other, need the love that comes from outside ourselves, the love of God that comes through the people he has chosen to give to us.

Some of us are given to one another in very special ways. Some hands reach out to each other as husband and wife, as God chooses a man and a woman for the particular relationship of a marriage. But our particular relationships are lived out in a larger community. And we all have important things to offer this incredible network of intertwined lives.

This community, this linking of one to another, is God's gift to us. That is where God's grace comes in. In grace God gives us the gift of community. And in grace, God promises to sustain that community.

The marriage rite of the *Lutheran Book of Worship* proclaims that truth in this way:

> *The Lord God in his goodness created us male and female and by the gift of marriage founded human community in a joy that begins now and is brought to perfection in the life to come. Because of sin, our age-old rebellion, the gladness of marriage can be overcast and the gift of the family can*

> *become a burden. But because God, who established mar-*
> *riage, continues still to bless it with his abundant and ever-*
> *present support, we can be sustained in our weariness and*
> *have our joy restored.*

Whether you are a very active member of a congregation or some-one who attends church only occasionally, you are reading this book because you want to be married by a pastor during a worship service. Rather than be married by a justice of the peace in a secular ceremony, you and your spouse-to-be have chosen to make God, and the church community, a part of your wedding.

That choice, in and of itself, reveals your hope and faith that this particular relationship you are in is a gift from God, a gift God has called you to accept with God's blessing.

But God's involvement in your marriage will not end when the wedding is over and you are walking down the aisle as husband and wife. That is the good news promised by the marriage rite quoted above and proclaimed by the whole Christian church. In God's grace, God will continue to be with you in all that lies ahead. As you share your joys and sorrows and all that the years will bring, God will be present, blessing and restoring you, so that you may fulfill the promises you will make on your wedding day.

How To Use This Workbook

This book is designed to introduce you to some basic relationship gifts or themes: intimacy, freedom, power, and security.[1] Each of these four gifts will be defined and explored, helping you to understand how God seeks to work in your life through these gifts.

In the process, you will be asked to reflect upon the expectations, hopes, and dreams you have regarding these gifts. As you begin this process of self-reflection, you will also be asked to enter into conver-sation with your spouse-to-be about his or her expectations, hopes, and dreams.

The expectations, hopes, and dreams you and your partner have are rooted in the experiences you each had in your family of origin, the family you grew up in. Whether you are conscious of it or not, the marriages of your grandparents, parents, and other relatives are mod-els for your thoughts on marriage. Furthermore, the way you interacted with your parents and siblings, how much you talked and shared, how you spent time together, etc., have helped to shape your expectations about how people live together. The starting point for this workbook, therefore, is an exploration of your family of origin and how it has influenced your understanding of life together.

This is an important part of your pre-marital preparation. You and your spouse-to-be have begun a journey together, and it is essential that you commit to the process of getting to know your life-long traveling companion! Your conversations will provide you with an opportunity to grow in understanding about yourself and each other, to notice and pay attention to your similarities and differences, and to enter the process of becoming a couple.

While you are exploring the four relationship themes, you will also be alerted to some of the challenges each marriage faces. As discussed above, we Christians live in the reality that relationships bring both gifts *and* burdens. Our sin — the insecurities, fears, failures, and weaknesses that each of us humans struggles with — often can turn something that is good and healthy into something painful and unhealthy.

A gift can thus become a burden, and we will draw your attention to the ways in which this can happen and to some of the tools you and your partner can use to take on those challenges together.

We hope that you will continue to use this book after your wedding day, as your relationship grows and changes. Your journey as husband and wife will offer lots of opportunities for conversation, reflection, learning, and love!

---

1. The four relationship themes were developed out of the clinical practice and teaching scholarship of Dr. Herbert W. Stroup, Jr., and Dr. Norma Schweitzer Wood. Dr. Stroup was Professor Emeritus of Pastoral Theology at Lutheran Theological Seminary at Gettysburg. Dr. Wood is Professor of Pastoral Counseling and Interpersonal Ministries at the same institution.

Chapter 2
Forming A New Family

Therefore a man leaves his father and his mother and clings
to his wife, and they become one flesh. — Genesis 2:24

Marriage, you've likely noticed, provides a wealth of material for humorists — and probably not without cause. Many in-law jokes poke fun at couples who are trying with little effect to fend off the unhelpful "wisdom" of their in-laws. These jokes remind us that it can be a struggle for each partner in a marriage to separate from his or her family of origin, the families we are born and raised in. Our families of origin often continue to pull on us, even after we're married, and competing loyalties can create stress. Some humorists focus on the "culture wars" within marriage — on those problems couples run into simply because their families of origin are quite different from each other.

Miss Manners provides a marvelous illustration of a family of origin "culture war" in her sympathetic account of a newly-married couple preparing for their first Christmas celebration[1]:

> *His family has always hung colored electric lights on everything they own, including the cat, the day after Thanksgiving; her family thinks three dull green satin balls on a living potted tree on the coffee table is as much as one can do to make the house festive without it being garish.*
>
> *Her family opens presents on Christmas Eve; his opens them on Christmas morning. His family always goes to late service on Christmas Eve; hers goes caroling.*
>
> *Her family sends cards only to faraway friends and checks off those received in a red notebook before sending them to a children's hospital; his sends cards to everyone, including next-door neighbors and live-in siblings and sticks those received in the slats of the Venetian blinds.*
>
> *His family gathers in New Hampshire for Christmas and expects them to be there; hers gathers in Chicago, and expects them to be there.*
>
> *Do you begin to see what chance this couple has of making it to the New Year?*

You may laugh as you read this and yet recognize something of yourselves in this scenario. For our families are indeed little cultures, and they each have their own values and rules of operation. Families are, in a sense, "founding" cultures for us, that is, they shape our basic views and experiences of reality and teach us about ourselves in relationship to others, about the world we live in, and about life's promises and challenges.

Your families of origin, therefore, are great influencers of the hopes, values, and standards that the two of you bring to your relationship and into your married life. You are no doubt aware of some of these influences. You may, for example, think it is good *and normal* to greet your spouse affectionately as you come and go during the day, as you've seen your parents do, and could well be surprised, disappointed, and frustrated if that thought is not shared by your spouse. You may have vowed to change some family patterns: you want the two of you to talk things out calmly and not slam doors or shout, as your parents did.

Every one of our families influences us in a subterranean way, below the surface, so that we don't know or even recognize its presence. These hidden understandings and expectations can create ongoing disruption and frustration in our relationships, even while, above ground, we are trying to love and faithfully care for one another.

This chapter and those that follow suggest that by studying your families of origin, the two of you will learn how to recognize situations where hidden expectations are creating marital burdens and frustrations, and come to understand your relationship even better than you do now.

Making A Genogram

Studying your families of origin begins with "the begats," that is, making a family chart. The chart or genogram serves as a map of your family of origin. A first step, then, is to take a sheet of paper and by your best recollection, put down who is in your family and when they were born, and record any deaths. Using squares for males and circles for females, begin with your maternal and paternal grandparents, add their siblings, spouses, and children; then move to your parents and add their siblings, spouses, and children. Place siblings in their birth order, moving from left to right. Finally put in dates of birth, marriage, divorce, and death. The genogram form on the next page provides a pattern for you as you draw your own chart, but you will have to adapt

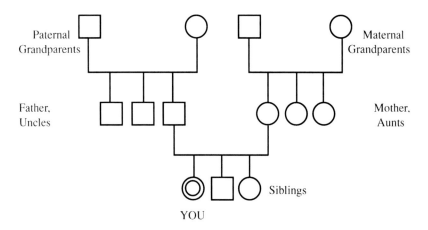

it to your own situation. If your parents divorced at some point in your growing up years, your family of origin may include stepparents and stepsiblings.

Once couples have charted out their family genograms, they often find that they are able to see family relationships and even patterns that they've never seen before. And the fiancé or spouse is often grateful for help in coming to know the in-law family.

Size And Shape

As we move through the following chapters you will be asked to return to your genogram to study your family from varying perspectives, but we begin now with how family culture is influenced by size and shape. With your genograms side by side, look at their relative sizes and shapes, and talk about what you notice. You might see that one of you comes from a larger or smaller family than the other. To give you an idea of how this works, we've included a sample from Melissa and Mark. (See page 18.)

Melissa observed that in her larger extended family there was always someone around to talk to, to share the work, to play with. "You bumped into or got a phone call from your aunt or uncle or cousin on a daily basis. You never got lonely, but there wasn't all that much privacy."

Mark's family provided considerable space and privacy. One of the first things he noticed about Melissa's home was the hustle-bustle always going on, and he commented that it's hard to keep track of all

Mark Wolfe's Genogram in 1997

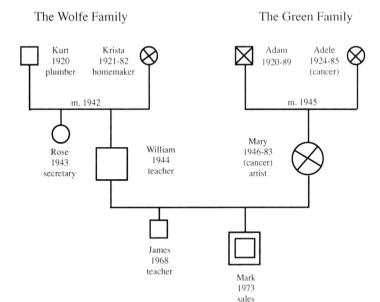

Melissa Brown's Genogram in 1997

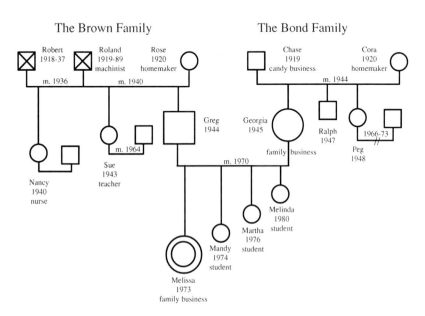

the conversations going on at once, especially on holidays when the whole family gathers. While Melissa shared a bedroom, clothing, books, and entertainment with at least one or more of her sisters, Mark had his own room because of the age difference between Mark and his older brother Jim. At his house, whoever is around at dinnertime eats together and catches up on how their days went.

The two family cultures were different beyond size. Mark's mother died when Mark was ten, leaving his father a single parent. After that, family life centered around the guidance and authority of his father who was given occasional help and advice from his sister, Mark's aunt. Mostly Mark went to his father if he needed help with something, or his brother Jim if he was around. He found himself at times lonely and wondering how life would be if his mother were still alive. By contrast, one or the other of Melissa's parents was always there, but by the time Melissa was eight, she learned that she'd get a more favorable response from her mother on some things and for other things she would go to her father. There was plenty of advice available for the asking from her aunts, uncles, and grandmother.

Melissa and Mark, then, can see differences in their family experiences of privacy, living space, and family interaction. As they prepare for marriage, Melissa and Mark should discuss how their different families of origin experiences in these areas have shaped each of their expectations for marriage.

Birth Order And Gender

In addition to the size and shape of our families, studies have shown that birth order and gender play an important role in the shaping our family culture and us. Often oldest children are given responsibilities to help with the younger children. As a result they develop leading and supervisory capabilities, in comparison to youngest born who often are "taken care of" by older siblings.

If you are interested in delving more into this subject, a good book to work with is *Birth Order and You: How Your Sex and Position in the Family Affects Your Personality and Relationships.*[2] For now, just notice what are some differences and similarities between the two of you. If you were the oldest, like Melissa, or the youngest, like Mark, talk about how that may have shaped your understanding of responsibility in a household and in your relationship with each other. Perhaps one of you generally takes the lead in making relationship plans and in getting things done around the house. It was helpful for Mark and Melissa to notice and evaluate their leading and following patterns. Melissa was in the habit of planning ahead and Mark of going along. Mark found that frequently the couple's schedule was filled so far in advance that he found himself without time for things that were important to him.

- Look at your patterns. Are both of you comfortable? Does anyone feel a bit burdened or pushed? Where and how? How might you improve on this?

- Now notice what were the roles of males and females in your families as you were growing up. Some families have a strict code of behavior, e.g., females do all the "inside-the-house" work, and males do all the "outside-the-house" work, while others make few distinctions, i.e., males do their share of cooking and cleaning and females take their turns at yard, car, and basement care.

- What difference did it make in your family that you were male or female? How are you now thinking about the division of responsibility in your relationship? Is gender a major factor here, or not?

Mark had no sisters and Melissa, no brothers, so they took time to talk about what it was like for each of them, admitting to some awkwardness and uncertainty in dealing with the other's brother and sisters.

Change And Loss: The Influence Of Life Events

All of us feel the impact of life changes, not just those changes that occur to and around us, but even those we ourselves decide on. We may feel frightened when illness and death happen to us and around us, or angered by events or changes that seem unfair; we may feel elated by love, marriage, the birth of a longed-for child.

We seek the positive changes in our lives, but when disappointments and losses happen, we use whatever resources we have to cope as best we can. Families too feel the impact of these changes and react to them in characteristic ways, according to the family's values, needs, and available resources. Some families respond to the loss of a loved one by reaching out to others for help, while others seem to keep within the family their expressions of pain and sadness.

Families develop their own traditions (a la Miss Manners) to mark transitions, some responding to joyous occasions with noisy and extravagant celebrations and others doing so with quiet, very private acknowledgments. One family celebrates birthdays with a week-long countdown marked with a surprise gift and card each morning and a large extended family party on the birthday itself. Another family skips gifts, cards, and parties, but has birthday cake together after a regular family dinner.

One thing is clear — major life events and transitions do shape the family culture as well. Adjustments in the way daily life is conducted have to be made — whatever the change, be it a birth, a marriage, a divorce, a death, a serious illness, promotion, loss of job, geographical move. Around each of these, responsibilities must shift, loyalties are stretched, and family bonds weakened or strengthened.

For example, when Mark's mother died of cancer, father and sons grieved deeply; family life was changed forever. Mark noticed that he suddenly grew up, his brother and father involved him in more responsibilities for himself and around the house, and a persisting sadness remained. They stopped going on vacations together and doing some other things associated with Mark's mother.

When Melissa's aunt divorced and moved away, this event not only upset the family equilibrium but also that of the family business. As close as the family was — there had been no inkling of trouble until the decision was made. They were stunned, as there had never been a divorce in the family. Upset, other family members responded to each other with much phoning and meeting and persuading and attempts to find ways to help. After much struggle and conversation, there were shifts in responsibilities and investments, such that Melissa's parents ended up buying out Aunt Margaret's share of the business and covering her responsibilities at work. The overall effect was that Melissa's family became further invested in the operation of this small family business with its time requirements and its economic ebbs and flows. The center of Melissa's family life seemed to shift to the store and its demands; her parents were busier with work. Melissa and her sister, at ages nine and eight, were also asked to carry a larger share of the homework and younger childcare. Melissa and her sisters still attended Sunday school each Sunday, but frequently now their parents were not free to be there with them.

- Now go to your own genogram again and think about what major changes have happened in your family's history and life over the last twenty years, for example. You've already recorded dates of births, marriages, deaths, and divorces. Now think about other changes, geographic moves, major illnesses or disabilities, job changes, etc. List these in the right hand corner of your genogram along with their dates.

- Now think about how your family reacted to these. What do you notice? When people are upset do they reach out to other family members, or do they pretty much handle things on their own?

- Think about one loss event, such as a death or separation. Did members express their feelings liberally and loudly or were they more private and contained about their feelings?

- Do the same thing with an event of celebration, such as a big achievement or a birth or even the announcement of your own marriage. How would you describe your family's way of responding?

- We'll be looking further into family reactive patterns in each of the next chapters. For now, share your noticings and discoveries with each other. If there are any observations that you think might be helpful to understanding your own relationship, mention these to each other for further consideration and reflection.

Family Values
Family values are those "goods" around which the family makes its choices and decisions about how to invest their resources of time, energy, commitment, talent, and money. Some families give great importance to education, others less so; some put financial success as the highest value, others prize simplicity and thrift; some are child-centered more than they are adult-centered or career-centered.

Noticing what the family rules are may give clues about what values operate in your family. Let's look at some of these, both spoken and unspoken. Take each of the following topics, and let the questions related to each get you started on describing your family's values. Jot down some notes and then, before you move to the next family value, take time to share with each other what you've thought about.

- Think about *education*. What was communicated to you about grades, subjects, programs, about learning in general? Was your schooling something your parents took more or less interest in? Perhaps there were rules in your family about when homework had to be done, or about grades and report cards. In Mark's family, for example, there was an unspoken rule that a college education was a must. Even though Mark had no idea of what he wanted to do after high school and wished he could take a year's break from schooling, he was expected to go on and get a college degree in something. In Melissa's family, this emphasis was missing, although they did not discourage Melissa's initiatives.

- What about *work*? What are the occupations in your family? How did they view their work? As something that had to be done in order to make a living? A satisfaction? A combination? What about work around the house? Who does what? What were your responsibilities? What rules ("Before you go out to play, watch TV, read that book, I want you to ...") and incentives (allowance, privileges, praise, punishments, and penalties) did your parents use to motivate you to carry out these responsibilities?

- What did you learn about the value of *money*? Were you encouraged to get a job to help pay for your own expenses? To help out the family? Did the family urge savings for a rainy day? What were the rules about paying cash or using credit cards?

- What about *religion*? Did your family practice a faith? Did you take part in a religious education program? What was communicated to you about religious days and holidays? How did your family regard Sundays, for example? What were the family traditions around Christmas? What are some of the values you hold as you plan for a meaningful wedding?

• Now, take time together to notice what are the similarities and differences in your families' values. Where are the two of you in relation to these values? The point of doing this — just to say it one more time — is that we tend to use our experiences in our families of origin to develop marital standards of what is right, wrong, and normal. By studying your families as cultures of influence, and noting the ways in which each of you is similar and different from your own family and from each other's, you are helping yourselves to form your own family unit. While sharing similarities tends to strengthen those values, differences are often challenging for couples to handle. For this reason it's important to recognize differences and begin to find ways to accept them or to collaborate to find solutions to the challenges your differences create. Noticing these areas of value similarity and difference is an important first step.

Summary

In this section we asked you to look at each of your families: who are the members; how each generation is composed in terms of size and shape; what are some of the major life events that helped to create a certain kind of family culture; and finally what were/are the family rules and values around education, work, money, and religion. In the next section, we'll use your genograms in exploring the subject of intimacy.

Prayer Exercise 1: Prayer can be listening, asking, thanking, praising, complaining, or all of these, addressed to God. Praying is fundamentally inviting God to be there and desiring God's guidance. Prayer exercises suggest particular ways for this inviting of God's presence and guidance.

Since in this chapter, we've been paying attention to how we bring our family experience to the union of marriage, slowly and prayerfully read over the following passages together.

Therefore a man leaves his father and his mother and clings to his wife, and they become one flesh.   — Genesis 2:24

Honor your father and your mother, as the Lord your God commanded you, so that your days may be long and that it may go

well with you in the land that the Lord your God is giving you.
— Exodus 20:12

The first home is one that all of us must let go of as we go forth to find new homes. And yet, we always carry it with us.
— Macrina Wiederkehr[3]

• How has God blessed *you* through your family of origin?

• Are there any experiences, values, or patterns, etc., from your family of origin that are troubling to you or that you wish to change as you form a new family culture with your partner? Where would you ask for God's strength and guidance?

------

1. *The Washington Post*, Sunday, December 20, 1981, H1.

2. *Birth Order and You: How Sex and Position in the Family Affects Your Personality and Relationships* is written by Lois and Ronald Richardson, published in 1990 by Self-Counsel Press, Vancouver.

3. Wiederkehr, Macrina, *A Tree Full of Angels: Seeing the Holy in the Ordinary*, Harper and Row, 1990.

Chapter 3
Intimacy — The Gift Of Presence,
The Burden Of Alienation

Human love takes its color from divine love. When we develop and express our love to another person we are using the same words and actions and emotions that are also used to develop and express our love for God, and to describe God's love for us.[1]

One important reason couples give for deciding to marry is that they love each other, feel close to one another, and want to stay close. You probably know what they mean. When you are together you feel connected to each other in some wordless way; at times your separate

"If something is bothering you about our relationship, Lorraine, why don't you just spell it out."

selves seem to melt into togetherness. Your bond with each other seems so strong, you want to build a future on it. It's exhilarating, surprising, and wonderful — this God-given gift of attraction and love. *God tells us that this gift in marriage is sacred and holy.*

It's hard to believe that the couple in the cartoon on page 27 might have once felt such a strong bond of connection. How could such distancing change have taken place? And yet all relationships are vulnerable to feelings of disconnection, though perhaps not as dramatic or comedic as this one. Nonetheless, those times of separation are disappointing and painful. And obviously this couple has not just a breakdown in communication, but also a clash of expectations regarding what their life together should be like.

In marriage two people are drawn uniquely together, out of a God-given yearning to be with one another and to live in relationship. At the beginning of love relationships, the lovers often marvel at the ways in which they are alike. They even enjoy the differences they notice. Mark and Melissa, for example, quickly discovered that they shared the same taste in music, movies, books, and friends; their mutual passion for environmental issues brought them together initially through a school club. While they were also aware of their different personalities, they seemed to complement one another. The fact that Mark was more quiet and Melissa more talkative seemed to make them a good fit.

But because a couple is made up of two unique people who are not clones of one another, inevitably what emerges are some differing expectations they have of the relationship and of each other. A partner's quiet approach in certain circumstances may disappoint the spouse's expectation for active support and involvement. Or an active, expressive style can be experienced as noisy and intrusive. When the characteristic that was so appealing in the past all of a sudden becomes annoying, the feeling of intimate connection may disappear, as the disappointed partner thinks, "Why can't s/he be more like me?" In the loneliness and separation of these moments, the relationship may feel like a burden. The challenge is to recognize that these disruptions of togetherness are perfectly normal. They can be expected in any relationship simply because each partner is an individual, uniquely a creature of God's. These times of separation signal to partners that they have a task before them: to find ways to understand their differences that will help them reconnect with each other.

What we want to do in this chapter is explore intimacy as a wonderful kind of glue in your relationship. To do that we begin by inviting you to think about some of your ideas, feelings, and expectations of marital intimacy.

Although intimacy has long been used as a term for sexual intercourse, it has a much broader meaning. It has been described as an intensely personal relationship of sustained closeness in which partners know and are known by each other, deeply and affectionately. This closeness respects the unique selfhood of each partner. Not surprisingly, hopes for intimacy are shaped by what people experienced in their family relationships. These formative experiences along with other significant relationships affect the way people express and experience intimacy in marriage. Let's look, then, at some of your learnings.

Ideally, families try to teach that intimacy is a balance of separateness and togetherness — that is, while each member of the family is a unique person, in age, role, and personality, each is connected to the whole family through a shared identity and sense of love and belonging.

But there is variety in expression from family to family which can be viewed on a continuum which differently emphasizes the values of individuality and togetherness.

INTIMACY

Being Close, Knowing/Being Known
Individuality - - - - - - - - - - - - - I/We - - - - - - - - - - - - - Togetherness

On the left of center on the intimacy continuum, family life emphasizes the individuality and independence of family members more than family unity and connectedness. Parents, as the architects of this family culture, care about personal space, privacy, and independence and feel less desire for family togetherness.

On the right of center, family life emphasizes family togetherness and belonging. A priority is placed on shared experiences and family loyalty.

The families of Mark and Melissa, whom we've already met, illustrate the two differing emphases on individuality and belonging. Because in Mark's family, people tended to do their own thing, keep most feelings to themselves, and solve their own problems, his picture of marital intimacy reflects many of these same experiences. Mark says he doesn't have to be in the same room with Melissa to be close to her; he feels close, he says, just knowing that she is in his life and that they will begin and end each day together. While Melissa values these book-end times of each day, her picture of marital intimacy includes many other moments of connecting and touching base with each other. Because in Melissa's family, people valued sharing of space, possessions, thoughts, and feelings, she looks for these same experiences in marriage.

Mark and Melissa have already had one argument involving these differing expectations:

> *It was a Sunday afternoon. Although they had not really talked about any plans, Melissa assumed that they would do something to share and relax over together. When she asked Mark when he was coming over, Mark replied that he had some things to take care of and would not be over until that evening after supper. Melissa was stunned at first, and then hurt and angry. They had so little time to see each other during the week, she couldn't imagine not wanting to spend time with the one you were planning to marry. Mark replied that just because there was so little personal time during the week he really wanted to take care of the list of chores that had piled up. He didn't know what she was making a fuss over. He'd see her in the evening.*
>
> *When Mark did come over later that day, Melissa, still hurt and feeling distant, tried to get the closeness back in the relationship by talking: What had happened? Where was Mark? Why had he suddenly not wanted to spend time with her? Did he realize just how disappointed and puzzled she was? Mark, having had time to take care of some personal things, felt sufficiently renewed by this alone time, and now was ready to do something with Melissa. He became annoyed that she seemed so hung up on this afternoon. He believed his actions had been perfectly reasonable and resented the suggestion on her part that he had been selfish and unloving. Furthermore, talking about this would get them nowhere. He believed they should just forget about it and move on instead of continuing to beat a dead horse.*

Because of your vantage point, you can see that in a sense both Mark and Melissa are "right" in wanting intimacy to be expressed in ways they are used to. It makes perfect sense for them to be thinking the way they are. But they are missing something important: an understanding of the other's perspective. Mark and Melissa need to be able to see each other's picture of intimacy, to understand the influence of family culture on their expectations and assumptions, and then, taking all of this into account, find ways to respond to and accommodate each other.

> Now, using the continuum and illustration above to pay attention to some of your assumptions and expectations about intimacy, take some time to read the questions below, ponder them, jot down some notes, and then share your thinking with your partner.

- What do you do to try to get close to your partner? How do you think your partner tries to get close to you?

- What is going on when you do feel close? Are there certain conditions that you feel need to be there in order for you to want to be close? Do certain situations lead to your feelings of closeness? Try remembering where you were the last time you felt really close to one another.

- What is going on when you don't feel close? Try remembering the last time you felt distant from your partner. What did it feel like? What did it mean to you?

- Are there times when you would like to understand your partner better or to be better understood? When are some of these?

- How do you let your partner know when you wish some time to yourself rather than be together? How does he or she let you know? Do the two of you come right out and say so or do you use non-verbal ways of trying to convey this?

- What did you learn about intimacy in your family culture? Do you see any connections between what you learned there and your expectations of each other?

Communication

You may have noticed, in doing the above exercise together, how important it is to communicate clearly and have a sense of whether you are connecting with or missing each other's meaning. Through sharing and listening people learn important details about each other, come to understand each other more fully, and experience closeness.

Communication specialists tell us that it is impossible for us not to communicate, because we human beings are always trying to make sense of whatever is going on in ourselves and around us. If you think about it, you've probably already noticed that even when your partner is silent, you try to interpret what the silence is saying to you: "Maybe she's mad at me" or "He's disappointed" or "She doesn't feel good" or "He doesn't really care."

Our interpreting tendencies, though — so useful in trying to understand the non-verbal behavior of infants and young children — can make communicating hard work. We can easily forget in our intimate relationships that we not only use language somewhat differently but, because we are not replicas of each other, we may make sense of things differently. To complicate things, people often magically think that "If s/he loved me s/he would know what I mean or what I want without my having to say it." We want so much to be understood and accepted for who we are, yet at times we struggle to make ourselves clear and hear the other person.

Communication about ourselves rarely involves the clear transmission from one person to another of an intended message that we suppose it does. (Because *I* know what I mean when I talk to you, I think *you* should know exactly what I mean.) Instead, communication usually involves an encoding process on the part of the speaker and a decoding process by the listener:

Speaker encodes - - - - - - MESSAGE - - - - - - Receiver decodes

A simple example would be: when she asks, "Are you coming home early tonight?" she may assume "early" to mean "before 5 p.m." He may translate "early" as 6 or 6:30, if he doesn't stop either to ask her what "early" means or to specify what hour he means.

When you think about what makes for clear and good communication between you and your partner, it's fairly easy to describe but not always easy to do. Paying attention to what you mean and how you are saying it and listening to your partner's responses are all basic steps in the process. This back and forth dance can be so smooth at times you don't even notice you are doing it. It's then all the more surprising when, for some reason, the dance falters or stops altogether.

• Noticing what makes for poor communication can be quite helpful in discovering what makes it better. You and your partner might explore this by selecting a topic to talk about for five minutes, such as how you'll spend your first vacation, or what would be an ideal weekend. During this time, use three poor communication tactics. You might try things such as looking away from your partner, looking bored, interrupting, not listening to what was being said, not talking yourself, not responding to what your partner says, attending to something else, yawning, etc. All of these behaviors signal lack of interest and lack of desire to know and be connected to each other. After five minutes, stop and talk about what it was like for each of you to employ these tactics. Did you recognize the other's tactics? What did it feel like to be on the receiving end? What was most disturbing to you?

• Now talk for five minutes on the same topic, but this time each of you use three communication strategies that you think will help you know and be connected to your partner. After five minutes, stop and again talk about what it was like.

• Compare your set of clear communication ideas with the list of guidelines below.

— Look at your partner and notice facial expressions, body language, and tone of voice.

— Use listening, acknowledging responses.

— Listen fully to what is being said before responding. Don't think about your response while your partner is still talking.

— Be open to the other's point of view, suggestions.

— Use "I" statements and be as specific as you can be about what you think, feel, and want.

— Paraphrase what you've heard.

— Check out your perceptions. (Am I sensing that you are annoyed?)

— Ask open questions. (Can you tell me more about that?)

— Avoid leading questions. (You know I'm right, don't you?)

— Don't escalate your voice to make your point.

— Don't cut your partner off.

— Don't criticize or argue with her or his experience. (You shouldn't feel that way! or What a dumb thing to think!)

— Sit so that you can see your partner's face when you are talking together.

— Put down the newspaper or book you are reading. Turn off the television.

You'll notice that most of these guidelines have to do with being a good listener. The saying, "Listening is 51 percent of good communication," is a way of making the point that listening goes beyond hearing and involves actively paying attention to the other person and what he or she is thinking and feeling.[2] Good listening gives a loving space for the partner to share his or her feelings, thoughts, and hopes.

PEANUTS reprinted by permission of United Feature Syndicate, Inc.

Empathy

Empathy, another way to build intimacy, is using your imagination to try to see what the world looks like and feels like in your partner's shoes. You no doubt already do this with each other out of a desire to be understanding and loving. Being empathic doesn't mean giving up your own perspective or your own feelings; it means making room for your partner's world of experience by trying to walk in her or his shoes a while and letting that affect you.

Marital communication often breaks down when empathy breaks down. And empathy seems to break down most when partners come up against their differences, or when they are sick or under stress. At the very time when empathy would help them understand each other, it seems to disappear. Differences sometimes do seem to threaten the bond of connection, as Mark's and Melissa's argument over expecting to spend time together illustrates. Melissa feels lonely and rejected and Mark feels criticized and misunderstood. Both feel the burden of alienation: Melissa, because her desire to have Mark share her experience is frustrated, and Mark, because he feels defensive and doesn't want to

Frank and Ernest

© 1980 Thaves / Reprinted with permission. Newspaper dist. by NEA, Inc.

get into an argument. Yet listening with empathy and letting your partner know that you understand her or him is not only a gift of love, but is also one of the most powerful tools for healing your relationship. Instead of criticizing or ignoring each other's point of view, the relationship can be healed if each partner makes an effort to listen empathically. Such an effort is a labor of love.

- Try to recall an experience when you really felt listened to, understood, and accepted for who you are. Tell your partner what this was like for you.

- Try to think of a time when you had difficulty understanding what was going on with your partner. See if you can explore what might help you get into his or her shoes. Sometimes it helps a lot to try imagining what is was like to grow up in your partner's family culture because it makes clearer why certain values are important to him or her.

A Protected Space For Your Relationship

One of the ongoing tasks in marriage is for the partners to define a clear and protected space for their relationship without ignoring or isolating themselves from friends, the rest of the family, and the world. In order to thrive, your relationship does need your attention, your time, and space. This means agreeing on some boundaries. When people set boundaries, they set "guidelines for" or "limits on" their responses to invitations and demands placed on them by work, family, friends, church, community involvements, and even hobbies.

Boundaries define your marital time, energy, and space; they are basically agreements and commitments which protect personal and marital space and your relationship's well-being.

The wedding marks a fundamental shift from a single lifestyle to a married one. Even the announcement of engagement lets people know that you are committing yourselves to each other and are not available for dating. When friends invite you for social occasions they know now to consider you as a couple. But there are also messages from family, friends, and even from work that seem to ignore the fact that your life has changed, that it is not business as usual:

- Both families may expect that you continue the tradition of coming to Thanksgiving dinner at their "home," ignoring the reality that you will need to establish traditions of your own. These new traditions will likely involve contact with both families, but the two of you will need to talk over and decide what to do and how.

- A brother may continue a pattern of dropping in to visit every Saturday afternoon without considering that the two of you have plans with each other.

- Friends may expect the same level of involvement in social activities and give you a hard time when you say you want to check with your spouse before saying yes or no to an invitation.

- Your place of work may not actually care what is happening in your personal life and simply expect that you will continue to give 110 percent of your time and energy. You may feel torn between what seem to be the demands of work and what is needed in your marriage relationship.

- If you are remarrying with children from a previous marriage, you may feel as though there just isn't enough of you to go around or that you are always having to choose between your children and your spouse, because each seems to expect more of you.

Decisions about protecting your relationship's time are made, of course, in light of the much larger picture of your outside relationships and responsibilities. What you most need as you make these decisions is a basic agreement to consult with each other as you are making plans, and to commit yourselves to your mutual benefit. We'll be looking more at how to do this in the next chapter.

There never seem to be enough hours in the day to do all that we hope to do. Getting married doesn't change this reality. In fact, when life gets busier, as it always does, couples start to give each other the leftovers of their hearts and minds. All too often these interactions become half-hearted and tired — after work, chores, calls, and visits with family or friends have depleted energy reserves. Spouses hope that tomorrow they'll feel more interested and loving with each other, but somehow tomorrow turns out to be just as busy and hectic as today.

One simple way of making daily space for your relationship is to build in a twenty or thirty minute time for touching base with each other. During this time every day, you give each other your undivided attention to find out what's going on in your worlds and emotionally reconnect to each other. Establishing such a ritual will involve some thinking and planning. Is it best to sit down together in the evening as soon as you come home, or could you be more attentive and relaxed after dinner, or later in the evening? Melissa and Mark decided to set aside time before dinner, because one or both of them could be scheduled to work in the evening at the family-run business. They could picture themselves sitting down together each weekday at 5 p.m. with their sodas and a basket of pretzels between them on the sofa, telling each other about the day and how it made them feel, and carefully listening to the other.

Sexual Intimacy

The desire to be close, connected, to know and be known may be experienced most profoundly in sexual intimacy, although even here partners' different expectations and understandings do come into play. These are some of the things that husband and wives say about intimacy:

> *Having sex with her makes me feel much closer so it makes it easier to bridge the emotional gap, so to speak. It's like the physical sex opens up another door, and things and feelings can get expressed that I couldn't before.*[3]

For me to be excited about making love, I have to feel close to him — like we're sharing something, not just living together ... I want to know what he's thinking, you know, what's going on inside him — before we jump into bed.[4]

It's the one time when I can really let go. I guess that's why sex is so important to me. It's the ultimate release; it's the one place where I can get free of the chains inside me.[5]

Yeah, but what it stands for; it's not just her. I mean, it's the contact with her, sure, but it's how it makes me feel. I guess the best word for that is "alive"; it makes me feel alive and I guess you could say, potent.[6]

I'm not always comfortable with my own sexuality because I can feel very vulnerable when I'm making love.[7]

Sometimes I can get scared. I don't even know exactly why, but I feel very vulnerable, like I'm too wide open. Then it feels dangerous. Other times, no sweat, it's just all pure pleasure.[8]

You can see from just these few quotations what a range of feeling and meaning can be expressed about sexuality and how important it is for partners to be able to reveal who they are to each other, to listen with empathy, and to respect each others' well-being.

One thing can be generally said, though: Close and loving sex usually flows out of a close and loving relationship overall. What goes on in the couple's daily life in the patterned ways of interacting with each other strongly influences feelings about themselves, about their relationship and desire to be close sexually. To say it another way, couples who *do not communicate* well with each other, *do not listen* to each other with interest and empathy, and *share little* in each other's daily lives, *cannot expect easily to connect sexually with each other.* Couples who experience loss in sexual desire often discover that they've stopped tending the relationship and allowed themselves to drift apart. General losses in intimacy affect the whole relationship including its sexual expression. But partners can also bring all of the gifts of intimacy to their sexual relationship and enjoy a deepening and a sustaining bond of love.

You want to remember that a book of the Bible, Song of Songs, is a collection of ancient, but beautifully composed, love poems in which the lovers talk openly about their tender love, their longing and desire for each other, and their lovemaking.

Summary
In one sense intimacy is a pure gift and blessing, not something we deserve or can control. But in another sense, we are responsible for caring for it, nourishing it in our relationships. In this chapter we've looked at what it might mean to nourish your marriage relationship: by becoming alert to expectations of intimacy which are affected by your family cultures; by paying attention to your habits of communicating with each other; by remembering and practicing the skill of empathy; by establishing a protected space in which you can nurture your relationship; and by recognizing loving sexuality as a marital gift.

Prayer Exercise 2: Prayer can be noticing ways that God expresses a loving relationship with us. Since in this chapter we've been paying attention to marital intimacy as knowing and being connected to each other, slowly read together the following part of Psalm 139 and notice how God's intimate knowing of us connects us to God and to life.

O LORD, you have searched me and known me.
You know when I sit down and when I rise up;
you discern my thoughts from far away.
You search out my path and my lying down,
and are acquainted with all my ways.
Even before a word is on my tongue,
O LORD, you know it completely.
You hem me in, behind and before,
and lay your hand upon me.
Such knowledge is too wonderful for me;
it is so high that I cannot attain it.

Where can I go from your spirit?
Or where can I flee from your presence?
If I ascend to heaven, you are there;
if I make my bed in Sheol, you are there.

If I take the wings of the morning
and settle at the farthest limits of the sea,
even there your hand shall lead me,
and your right hand shall hold me fast.
If I say, "Surely the darkness shall cover me,
and the light around me become night,"
even the darkness is not dark to you;
the night is as bright as the day,
for darkness is as light to you.

For it was you who formed my inward parts;
you knit me together in my mother's womb.
I praise you, for I am fearfully and wonderfully made.
Wonderful are your works; that I know very well.

No one can know and love us as profoundly as God, who creates us and gives to us the gift of intimacy in marriage and community.

---

1. Peterson, Eugene, *Five Smooth Stones*, John Knox, 1980, pp. 28 and 40.

2. Wolvin, Andrew and Coakley, Carolyn Gwynn, *Listening, 5th edition*, Brown & Benchmark, 1996, p. 68.

3. Rubin, Lillian, *Intimate Strangers: Men And Women Together*, Harper and Row, 1990, p. 104.

4. Rubin, p. 101.

5. Rubin, p. 106.

6. Rubin, p. 107.

7. Rubin, p. 107.

8. Rubin, p. 109.

Chapter 4
Power — The Gift Of Collaboration, The Burden Of Hoarding

The word "power" brings to mind many different images. When we hear that word, we often think of "powerful" people — movers and shakers on Wall Street, politicians in Washington, movie stars in Hollywood whose faces appear on the covers of magazines.

But power is something all of us humans seek to have in our lives. Having power means having the ability to influence what's happening in our lives and relationships. When we have power, we have some effect on our world — making things happen we want to have happen ... or keeping things we *don't* want to happen from happening.

None of us has absolute control over our world. For instance, we can try to stay healthy, eating right, getting exercise, not smoking or drinking to excess, seeing a doctor regularly. But, even if we do all those things, it's still possible that we will get sick, even very sick.

That's part of being human. We are never completely in control of our world. But how we choose to deal with that reality varies from person to person. Some people try to exert power over everything and everyone they can, in order to keep as much under control as possible. Some people just give up, feeling so powerless that they stop caring about trying to influence their surroundings in a direct way.

Most people aren't at those extremes. Each of us has our own individual attitude toward power, and our use and misuse of power falls somewhere along the spectrum shown below.

POWER

Having effect and influence

power over		powerless
hoarding, forcing - - - - - - - sharing - - - - - - - being underhanded		
authoritarian	give and take	passive/aggressive

Someone towards the left of the spectrum will tend to want to exert more control over life around him/her. This person may make more decisions on his or her own, always looking to get the upper hand or the advantage. For instance, Sue accepted a promotion at work, without discussing it with her husband Rick. It meant a bigger salary, more benefits, greater responsibility. It also meant that she'd be working more hours, be on call two weekends a month, and have to travel more.

The promotion was a dream come true for Sue. She assumed the money and status would give Rick and her an edge on their friends; that, in the long run, any objections Rick had to the long hours and travel would be overcome; and that he'd simply accept these changes in their home life and accommodate them.

Someone more on the right of the spectrum sees little opportunity to influence his/her world directly. Decisions seem always to be made by others, so this person develops different techniques for affecting the people and events around him or her. Rick felt powerless in this way. When Sue came home and told him about her promotion, he was hurt and angry that he hadn't been consulted or even considered. He didn't tell Sue this, however, or ask her to reconsider. Instead, he withdrew from Sue and didn't congratulate her on this accomplishment or share her excitement. He didn't say much at all, actually. Even when Sue pushed him to tell her if something was wrong, or if he was angry, Rick denied it, simply said that he wasn't feeling well, and went to bed early.

In a marriage, partners try to influence each other and their married life every day. From the big issues — will they buy a house? — to the small — who will take out the garbage? — a couple interacts in a unique way all the time to affect what will, or will not, happen in their life together. In making these decisions, partners need to learn how to share power.

As you recall from earlier chapters, many of the expectations and understandings we have about significant relationship gifts come from our experiences in our families of origin. The same is true for the gift of power. We learn about power first by seeing and experiencing how our parents, siblings, and other relatives use or misuse their power and how they respond to other people's use or misuse of power.

It is easier to see how people think about power in a situation of crisis — when they try to manage a situation in which they feel powerless. Let's take another look at Mark and Melissa and the way each family responded to a family crisis. When Mark's mother died, Mark was only ten years old. At a very young age, Mark lost one of the two most important people in his life. During his mother's last months of illness, he felt scared and helpless. No matter how much he and his father and brother loved his mom, no matter how many times a day they prayed for her or read her stories or brought her a glass of water, Mark's family could not make her get better.

Although he could not put it into words at the time, Mark can identify now the feeling he had after his mother's death: it was the feeling of absolute powerlessness. And it was a feeling shared by Mark's father and brother. Mark became less talkative, less likely to let people know, in a direct way, what he was thinking, feeling, and questioning because, in his mind, what he thought and felt didn't seem to have much effect on what was happening in his world.

Because his mother died while he was young, Mark can't remember much about how his mother and father made decisions about family matters like money and discipline. He knows, however, that, after the death, there wasn't much in the way of conversation between his father, brother, and him about their life. They didn't have "family conferences," or anything like that, where each family member could help make decisions about vacations, household responsibilities, etc. Mark remembers, though, that after his mother's death, his aunt often strongly voiced her opinion about important issues, and, for some reason, her opinion usually influenced how Mark's father made decisions.

Melissa's experience was a little different. When a family crisis occurred, like the divorce of her aunt, people responded assertively and shared power among themselves. Obviously, they couldn't change the fact of the divorce, but they responded to the consequences of the divorce decisively. Melissa's parents bought the aunt's share of the business and involved themselves in its operations. The lives of all of Melissa's family members were changed forever — priorities shifted, financial stability became less sure, time was invested in different ways — but, together, they put a positive spin on the changes. There were simply new challenges to be faced.

Melissa looks back on this as a learning experience. She realizes now that her family taught her "not to sweat the stuff she can't control," to worry only about the stuff she can control. And because her mother and father both were involved in the decisions about investing and working in the business, and were sensitive to the impact the business had on the rest of the family, Melissa has pretty clear expectations about how marriages should work: there should be a lot of give and take, discussion, compromise, teamwork.

A spouse's expectation about how decisions are made by a couple will be shaped by crisis experiences like Mark's and Melissa's, but also by the patterns and routines that get established in everyday life. They often are shaped also by birth order or gender. The youngest child in a family is sometimes "babied," given less power and responsibility than other family members. He or she then does not have much opportunity to develop decision-making skills, or enter into the "give and take" kind of negotiating that other children might do. On the other hand, the oldest child may have been given lots of power and responsibility at an early age. He or she may have gotten used to being an authority figure for the younger children, a babysitter, the "parental" figure when the parents weren't around.

A person growing up in a very "traditional" family may be affected by how gender roles were played out. Making decisions about money, career, cars, and vacations may have been seen as the job of the "man" of the household. Making decisions about how the children were disciplined or how the house was taken care of may have been seen as "woman's" work. Each had his/her own "turf," so to speak.

> Now, take some time to think about your family of origin, your decision-making process, and your expectations for how you and your spouse-to-be will work out the details of your life together.

- How were decisions made in your family? Did your parents make the decisions about family matters on their own? Were the children involved in discussions about family matters like moving, vacations, how they would be disciplined, whether they would get an allowance, etc.? Did you have "family conferences" where important topics were discussed? Did Mom and Dad make decisions for you (and your siblings)?

- Was one parent the final authority figure for the family? Did your parents divide decision-making on the basis of traditional gender roles? (i.e., Did your father take care of the finances and your mother take care of day-to-day decisions?)

- Did you see your parents disagree? Do you know how your parents worked out differences of opinion? Did one parent defer to the other when there was disagreement? Was it always the same parent, or did it depend on the issue?

- What kinds of decisions were you allowed to make for yourself? Were you allowed to spend your money the way you wanted to? Choose your own career or college? Were you given the power and freedom to buy your own clothes or pick the extracurricular activities you wanted to do?

- What did you do when you disagreed with your parents about something? Were you given the opportunity to talk it out? Did your parents have the final say?

- How do you make decisions now? How do you and your spouse-to-be make decisions together? Does one of you make decisions about certain things, for example, what you do in your time together or what kind of wedding you'll have? What happens when you disagree about something? Does one of you defer to the other? Is one of you more likely than the other to want to talk things out? Does it depend on the issue?

Conflict

When two unique individuals both try to have some influence over what's happening in their life together, there are bound to be times when disagreements occur. One spouse wants the house to be neat — he is bothered by clutter and is disturbed when the mail piles up, the dishwasher isn't run, and the kids' toys are scattered all over the living room. The other spouse could care less about this — she is perfectly content with a little bit of disorder as long as the place isn't actually dirty.

The graph on the next page helps us to picture some of the ways we tend to respond to situations involving conflicts of interest.[1] We often feel pulled in two directions and feel pressure to make a choice between asserting what we want and cooperating with what the other wants. The graph depicts five ways of responding to this uncomfortable tension.

CONFLICT RESPONSES

Focus	Competing	Collaborating
on		
Self	Compromising	
	Avoiding	Accommodating

Focus on Other

Avoiding the problem is often done by a person who tends to have feelings of powerlessness. This person isn't confident that he can influence the situation, or he's afraid of confronting the problem, so he simply doesn't deal with it openly. Sometimes, however, avoidance is a healthy response to a conflict; after all, not every situation is worth the time and energy it would take to try to change it. If, when your spouse uses your car, he always reprograms the radio to stations you hate and never remembers to change it back, instead of confronting him about it, you may simply decide to let it go. Maybe next time he'll remember, you say (to yourself, one hopes!).

Accommodation occurs when one person allows the other to make a decision he or she is not thrilled with. The accommodating spouse "gives in," in a sense. Think back to Sue and Rick. After a few days of giving Sue the silent treatment, Rick decided that, because Sue's promotion was so important to her, there wasn't much he could do to change her mind about accepting it. Even though he knew that they'd have less time to spend together, and a more stressful life, Rick wanted to keep the peace. He'd give up the "couple time" that was so important to him if it made Sue happy.

Competition occurs when one person is convinced that his or her way is the "right" way to do something. There is no real discussion of the issue and no consideration of what the other spouse is feeling or thinking, just an arguing for his or her way. The competitive spouse will try to impose the decision on the other; if the other does not agree,

GOURMET COOK OF THE YEAR

". . And I'd like to thank my husband . .

This might be carrying accommodation a little too far!

a "battle" can develop. The two spouses may reach a stalemate, but often, at this point, the competitive spouse finds it hard to back away from the fight, because doing so means "giving in," letting someone "win." This pattern of competition can escalate so that spouses lose a sense of joint partnership and instead harbor feelings of hostility and resentment.

Compromise involves finding a way to meet some of the needs or wants of each partner, but not all. Both people decide what's most important to them and what they can live without or put up with in order to find some resolution to a conflict. For example, Joan doesn't want to go to Jim's company picnic; she'd rather spend a beautiful, relaxing day hiking around the local state park. Jim knows everybody else's spouses will be at the picnic; he also never has shared Joan's love of the outdoors. As a compromise, Joan agrees to go with him to the picnic, as long as they only stay an hour. In return, Jim will go for a short walk with Joan later that afternoon. Neither of them are completely satisfied with their plan, but are willing to accept it for the sake of their relationship.

Collaboration is by far the most difficult conflict resolution technique. It requires people to understand both what they themselves really want and what their partner wants. It also requires people to be creative — to find a way to respect and honor both sets of wishes or values. When Carol and Charles got married, they began a whirlwind of family holiday celebrations. After a few years of exhausting Thanksgivings and Christmases spent driving back and forth — mornings at Carol's parents, dinners at Charles' and then vice versa — Carol and Charles sat down to talk about the situation. After discussing what was really important to each of them, they decided that they would have dinner parties for each of their families of origin during the week between Christmas and New Year's, addressing their wishes to spend time with their families over the holidays. They'd alternate Thanksgivings, one year at Carol's, one year at Charles', in order to hold on to some of the traditions they each loved from their past. Christmas Day would be spent at home, with an open house for friends and neighbors in the afternoon. Carol's desire to be in a house full of people on Christmas would be met, and Charles' wish to start new traditions of their own would be satisfied.

As an introduction to the collaborative process, take some time to work on the following conflict resolution exercise.

1. Select one or two conflicts the two of you have had in the past.

2. Try to determine whether this is a misunderstanding or a disagreement.

   Misunderstanding: "I thought you meant this, but discovered as we talked that you meant that" or "I just assumed when I heard you talking on the phone that you intended to ... but as we talked I realized that I had taken what you said out of context" or "When I saw you frowning at me, I thought you were angry with me and didn't know, until you told me later, that you had a headache."

Disagreement: "I want to invite my mother to Thanksgiving dinner with us and you want us to eat alone" or "I want to relax after dinner with a newspaper and clean up later and you want to get the dishes done, the food put away as soon as we're done eating" (in other words, you understand each other very well, but disagree about an issue or area).

3. If your conflict was in fact a disagreement, at what step in the process toward negotiation and reconciliation did you stumble or get blocked?

4. Identify the issues of disagreement.

5. Decide on a time to discuss these.

6. Take turns hearing each person's perspective. What does each person want? Why?

7. Check that each has accurately heard the other's perspective.

8. Brainstorm about alternatives. (This is a time for creativity!)

9. Consider prayerfully what the two of you are discussing.

10. Make a decision and plans for future review and evaluation of your joint decision.

Power And Anger

As we've seen in this chapter, power is the issue which involves feeling like we can make a difference, that we have some influence over the things that happen to us and around us. When we have power, we feel like we can make happen the things we want to happen, or prevent the things we don't want to happen from happening.

Anger is related to the issue of power in an important way. People get angry because they care. You have hopes and expectations for your marriage and for your spouse — you have invested a lot of yourself in this relationship and will continue to do so as time goes on.

You care. And that means that sometimes you will get angry. After all, the opposite of "anger" is actually "apathy" — simply not caring

"Since we're both so tired, let's just reheat last night's argument."

enough to even be concerned about something or someone. Anger tells us that we're feeling like our hopes and expectations haven't been met. Something has happened or not happened in this important relationship that has hurt or disappointed us.

Anger in and of itself is not bad. Even the Bible recognizes it as a very natural thing — Cain, Moses, God, and Jesus all got angry.

We can't really control whether we have feelings of anger. Those feelings often come very quickly, as a reaction to something someone says or does or to a situation in which we find ourselves.

We *can* make choices, however, about what we do with our anger. We can vent it ("get it off our chest"). We can try to launch a counter-attack, striking out at whomever or whatever has provoked our anger. We can withdraw into ourselves, refuse to speak, bottle it all up inside.

The problem with these ways of dealing with anger is that they aren't very constructive. The feeling we have is expressed somehow, but we don't deal with the issue that made us angry in the first place!

When you vent or withdraw or lash out, you don't do anything to help fix the relationship you obviously care so much about.

To make matters worse, anger often feeds anger. You get hostile and take it out on your partner, and then your partner is hurt and takes it out on you! *Of course when anger leads to physical violence, this is never acceptable.* Violence not only destroys conditions that allow for trust and intimacy to flourish, but it seriously endangers personal safety.[2]

When verbal battles get started, you find yourself trying to "win" while making your partner "lose."

There is another choice. Anger can be used to build up your relationship, to help it grow. This happens when you identify what's making you angry (what's the underlying disappointment or hurt?) and communicate that to your partner. Then ... you can start collaborating to make it better.

Anger can be a very powerful tool for good. Anger can lead us to work for justice, to fight things like prejudice or hunger or poverty. It can inspire us to change what we believe is wrong or contrary to what God wishes for people.

When anger is used to fight wrong, it's what Saint Paul calls "speaking the truth in love." Paul recognized that we will become angry at times and warns us to "[b]e angry, but do not sin.... Put away from you all bitterness and wrath and anger and wrangling and slander, together with all malice, and be kind to one another, tenderhearted, forgiving one another" (Ephesians 4:26, 31-32).

Anger tells us that something in our relationship needs attention or work. Addressing that issue kindly and lovingly can lead to positive change and a deeper relationship as you grow in understanding of one another's needs and dreams. By "speaking the truth in love," you build up your relationship, rather than tear it down.

Speaking the truth in love and using anger constructively leads to a win/win situation. And this way of dealing with our spouse calls for forgiveness. Forgiveness ends that process of retaliation, of hurting one another to "get back" at each other. The forgiveness we offer also helps our partner want to work with us on our relationship.

All of this is rooted in God's love for us. There are lots of stories in the Bible about God's anger at our disobedience. God cares about and loves us enough to get frustrated when we turn away. But God is always forgiving us and calling us back to a deeper relationship. Through that relationship, God then gives us the strength and courage to love and forgive and build up the people in our lives.

Anger Exercise: Take a few moments to answer the following questions. See how you deal with/react to anger and then talk about your answers with your partner.

1.   What words or pictures come to mind when you try to describe anger?

2.   How did your parents express their anger toward you and toward each other?

3.   What conflict management styles did they tend to use? Avoiding, competing, accommodating, compromising, collaborating?

4.   How did other members of your family deal with anger and conflict?

5.   Describe what your feelings were when someone was angry with you.

6.   How did your family react when you got angry?

7.   How do you react when your partner is angry?

8.   Do you respond any differently when s/he is angry with you?

9.   How do you let your partner know that you are angry?

10. How do you let her/him know that you are "over" your anger?

11. Are there other feelings you associate with being angry?

12. How would you describe yourself? As slow or quick to anger? As one who holds a grudge or is quick to forgive and forget?

These questions are adapted from *Couples in Treatment: Techniques and Approaches for Effective Practice*, Gerald R. Weeks and Stephen Treat, Brunner/Mazel, 1992.

Prayer Exercise 3: Prayer can help us let go of our hurts and resentments, as we ask God for strength and guidance. Read slowly together the words of this passage from Matthew's Gospel:

Then Peter came and said to him, "Lord, if another member of the church sins against me, how often should I forgive? As many as seven times?" Jesus said to him, "Not seven times, but, I tell you, seventy-seven times."

"For this reason the kingdom of heaven may be compared to a king who wished to settle accounts with his slaves. When he began reckoning, one who owed him ten thousand talents was brought to him; and, as he could not pay, his lord ordered him to be sold, together with his wife and children and all his possessions, and payment to be made. So the slave fell on his knees before him, saying, 'Have patience with me, and I will pay you everything.' And out of pity for him, the lord of that slave released him and forgave him the debt. But that same slave, as he went out, came upon one of his fellow slaves who owed him a hundred denarii; and seizing him by the throat, he said, 'Pay what you owe.' Then his fellow slave fell down and pleaded with him, 'Have patience with me, and I will pay you.' But he refused; then he went and threw him into prison until he would pay the debt. When his fellow slaves saw what had happened, they were greatly distressed, and they went and reported to their lord all that had taken place. Then his lord summoned him and said to him, 'You wicked slave! I forgave you all that debt because you pleaded with me. Should you not have had mercy on your fellow slave, as I had mercy on you?' And in anger his lord handed him over to be tortured until he would pay his entire debt. So my heavenly Father will also do to every one of you, if you do not forgive your brother or sister from your heart."

— Matthew 18:21-35

- Talk with each other about your reactions to this parable.

- It's been said that what irritates us about others is the very thing we don't like in ourselves. It helps to remember that God's forgiveness of our faults and flaws releases us to forgive others.

1. This graph of conflict responses is based on the model developed by Kenneth W. Thomas and Ralph H. Kilmann cited in *Family Communication: Cohesion and Change*, 3rd edition, edited by Kathleen M. Gavin and Bernard J. Brommel, Harper Collins, 1991, p. 176.

2. For more on domestic violence, an excellent resource is *Women Healing and Empowering*, published in 1996 by the Evangelical Lutheran Church in America Stop The Violence Project. The Domestic Violence Hotline is 1-800-787-SAFE.

Chapter 5
Security — The Gift Of Commitment, The Burden Of Anxiety

*Marriage at its best is loving and life-giving. This relation-
ship grows and changes over time through experiences of
brokenness and healing, joy and failure, pressures and play,
forgiveness and renewal. It is truly a safe space — physi-
cally, emotionally, and spiritually — where each person feels
free to be vulnerable.*[1]

**"... with your promises bind yourselves to each other as
husband and wife."**

When, during your wedding ceremony, you make promises of faithfulness to each other, you and your partner will bind yourselves together and create a safe space. You will "tie the knot" and each promise
to the other that — come what may — rough times, adversity — I
intend to stay with you and keep sharing with you in good faith and
trust. In marriage, each of you makes a commitment to work things
through when the gladness of marriage is overcast.

While these mutual promises do create a climate of trust and safety
in marriage, they cannot eliminate all the sources of insecurity and
anxiety. Insecurity and anxiety affect all of us as we come face to face
with the limits of life, the sense of our own fragility, and the knowledge that, in addition to joy and happiness, pain and suffering may too
be in our future.

Each partner may think about security in slightly different ways.
These differences may be influenced by values related to body size,
health, gender, family culture, religious beliefs, and life experiences.
However different these ideas are, though, one reality is the same: when
our security is threatened or lost, we all get anxious. In fact, security
and anxiety can be seen as the flip sides of each other: security is the
relative freedom from anxiety, and anxiety is a loss of security.

Anxiety is an unsettling experience, whether it comes in the form of
a mild and vague sense that something is not quite right or a full-blown,

heart-pounding, adrenaline-rushing panic. Anxiety usually shows up when we think our well-being is being threatened and recedes when the threat goes away. Uncomfortable as it is, anxiety can be helpful. It can alert us to potential harm and energize us to fight off danger or to move away from it. It often stimulates us to solve problems and develop coping strategies, because it drives us to reinstate security as best we can.

Anxiety comes out most strongly in times of crisis and loss: when someone we love gets very sick or dies or leaves us or when accidents, disasters, or violence affect us and the people we love most. But even lesser stress and life changes may create anxiety: doing a difficult job, moving, marrying, having a baby, even disagreeing with one another. Here the anxiety may be mingled in with other feelings — pride, joy, eagerness, satisfaction, annoyance and so can go unrecognized. The result may be behavior that appears puzzling and uncaring to your partner.

In this section, then, we want to focus on your perceptions of both security and anxiety since both affect the life of your marriage.

Most of us find Linus and his security blanket amusing and even a little comforting. Even as we smile, we know exactly what it feels like to have a security blanket as well as to have it snatched away. Our "security blankets" may be a little more subtle and sophisticated because we've had more years than Linus to develop practices of coping

PEANUTS reprinted by permission of United Feature Syndicate, Inc.

with anxiety and settling ourselves down when we get "hyper." And we've been influenced by the examples of those close to us.

When we feel anxious and thrown off balance, we often do one of two things to get back our footing and secure ourselves: we look to others' help and support, and we look to ourselves to find some order, meaning, and a way to cope.

Both responses can be very helpful. In fact, we may do a little of both. If you learn that you have been diagnosed with cancer, or that you are in danger of losing your job, you will probably both seek help from others *and* dig into your own resources to bring some order to the world of chaos surrounding you.

Because of all the influences that shape us — our nervous system, our family of origin experiences, and critical life events — most of us lean toward one or the other response without even being aware of it.

SECURITY

Anxiety - - - - - - - Relative Absence of Threat - - - - - - - Anxiety
Fear of chaos   Fear of abandonment
Response is creating   Response is dependence on
good order   partner or security "stuff"

The continuum above shows these two tendencies, one at each end with a combining of the two tendencies at the center.

On the left side, the major threat to security is chaos — that feeling of not knowing what will happen next, being caught up in a swirl of confusion and disorientation. The response to this kind of anxiety is to fight off the threat of chaos by trying to get good order into life. The world of chaos was pretty much what it was like for Mark after the death of his mother. Life changed in an instant, with no warning. There was no sense to it. Mark asked why this happened to *his* mother, to *him*. His father's broken heart scared him, and his brother seemed to be in his own world. The situation was confusing and frightening: What on earth was going on? What did it all mean? And as scary as it was to be by himself, it was even worse having to be with his father and watch him collapse with grief.

Over time, Mark discovered that he felt somewhat better as he began to stay in his own room, his own space. He began to rearrange his room; as he did, it took his mind off his family's misery, and in some strange way created some space of peace and calm. He went through the family's collection of photographs, and carefully put pictures in chronological order. He cleaned up his closet and put aside games and books and toys that he felt he had outgrown. He even alphabetized the books in his bookcase. Though he could not have said it at that time, looking back, he can see that this getting some order into life was part of his coping with the profound anxiety and grief he felt over the loss of his mother and life as he knew and loved it. This way of coping has become a kind of pattern or ritual for him: when he feels down or unsettled, spending some time alone, getting life in good order always seems to help him feel more in control.

Mark is typical, then, of the left side of the continuum. He tends to rely on himself and his own resources to bring some order to his chaotic world. In doing so, he feels less anxious. There are many things we may do when we feel anxious to try to bring good order into our lives: we make lists of things to do; we store away things we think we might need someday even if we don't really need them now and throw out things that we think are cluttering up; we clean; we follow little rituals (first this, then that); we make sure doors and cabinets are closed, pictures are hung straight, and table surfaces are clear.

There is nothing wrong with any of these coping devices unless they begin to interfere with our relationships. If Mark spends so much time and energy on trying to get good order in his life that he ignores who Melissa is and what she is expressing to him, then a relationship problem is created. As it is, Mark's periodic retreat within himself to reorder things can be accepted by Melissa once she understands it as a response to his feeling that things are too chaotic and out of control.

On the right side of the continuum, the major threat to security is feeling weak, all alone, and helpless. The response to this kind of anxiety is to try to secure attachments to others, especially those who seem strong, reliable, and protective. Melissa, you may have guessed, illustrates this end of the continuum. And again, her family of origin experience has been influential. You will recall that she grew up in a larger extended family where people were always around for company and to lend a hand. When she was hurt or upset, someone was there to offer comfort and help. She and her sisters were taught to share with each other and that family members took care of each other. That's why it was a blow to the whole family when Melissa's aunt divorced, abandoned her interest in the family business, and moved a half-continent away. Everyone felt puzzled and hurt. The phone was perpetually in use after Aunt Margaret made her announcement, as the family reacted to this upsetting news by talking with each other about all that had happened. Finally they pulled together, reminded themselves that they still had each other, and Melissa's parents moved in to pick up the slack.

Because of her past experiences, security for Melissa centers on how stable her relationships of sharing and caring are. When she senses any distance and detachment in her relationship with Mark, she feels anxious about it. The worry sets in and stays like an upset stomach until her sense of loving attachment to Mark is restored. Her anxiety expresses itself as a preoccupation with being with Mark, talking things over, getting reassurance that he still loves her and is committed to the relationship. When carried to an unhealthy extreme this tendency to seek partner reassurance can result in a jealous possessiveness; in this case, to the jealous person the partner's normal interest in other people signals danger and potential abandonment.

As Mark better understands Melissa's experience of disconnection and her desire for reassurance, he can respond more sensitively. But you can see that while Mark's and Melissa's definitions of security (good order and reassurance of the partner's dependability, respectively) are not incompatible with one another, their tendencies when feeling anxious may present difficulties for the relationship. Mark's tendency to distance from the relationship to focus on his own desire for good order moves at cross purposes with Melissa's tendency to focus more intensely on the relationship to receive reassurance and support. Unless they come to notice these tendencies, understand what they mean, and try to work with each other, they may get caught like a "dog chasing its own tail." A vicious cycle could develop in which the more Mark distances, the more Melissa will pursue him, and the more Melissa pursues, the more Mark will distance.

> Using the continuum and illustration (pages 58 and 59) to notice some of your ideas about security and your anxieties, read the following questions below, jot down some notes about your observations, and then share your thinking with your partner. Perhaps as you talk together, you will better understand and cope with the expressions of security and anxiety in your relationship.

- What did you learn about security in your family culture? (You can get at this question, too, by thinking about your family's biggest worry.)

- Do you see any connections between what you learned there and your expectations of your partner?

- Were there any "events" in the life of your family similar to the death of Mark's mother or Melissa's aunt's divorce and move away? How did these affect you?

- How did you know when members of your family were worried? Did they tell you or did you notice certain changes in the way they behaved?

- What do you think you worry about most?

- What do you do about it to try to make yourself feel calmer and less anxious?

- Is there something, someone, some activity you think might operate as your "security blanket"?

- What do you think your partner worries most about?

- How do you know when she/he is anxious and worried?

- How do you try to make things safe again with each other?

- Do you see any similarities between the two of you in the ways you manage anxiety? Do you see any differences?

- Thinking about your responses to the questions above, identify at least two things you think might be key to maintaining trust and stability in your relationship.

Marital Comfort Zones

Marital comfort zones are those places of fit between our own ideas, values, and ways of doing things, and our partner's acceptance of them. The more alike partners' comfort zones are, the less stressful life in relationship may be. But there are always some areas of difference. You know how it is — you get cold when the thermostat goes below 70 degrees and your partner gets hot when it goes above 68. It does help to identify what exactly these zones are and explore some ways to accommodate each other. Though these differences may jostle us, paying attention to them helps build security in the relationship.

One story has it that some porcupines were spending a frigid winter night together. They discovered that in moving closer together they could get more comfortable by sharing their body warmth. If they got too close to each other, though, they felt the jab of each other's needles. After a series of trials — moving away and then close — they discovered a "right and proper" way to benefit from each other's warmth without being stuck by the other's needles. They found a mutual comfort zone.[2]

Here are three scenarios, each one describing a common relationship situation in which individual comfort zones are jostled. See if you find yourself identifying with any of these situations, then share your reactions with your partner.

"Shaker Simplicity" and "English Clutter"
It had been a long, busy day at work and Alex looked forward to home, supper, and an evening of unwinding and relaxing. He walked into the kitchen and thought, "What a mess." On into the dining room and the living room — not a clear surface anywhere. Books and magazines, a dish of quarters saved for the laundromat, some knickknacks that Amy collected, the children's toys, folded laundry on the steps, mail on the hall table. He longed for an uncluttered space, well-ordered calm, without the constant reminders of responsibilities. He just needed to relax and couldn't find a place to do that. Amy walked in the door soon after, only to hear, "This place is a mess! Look at it. How can you stand it? Can't we do something about it?" Amy, too, had had a busy day and was thinking how glad she was to get home.

It was cozy and warm, with all the reminders of family and things she loved. Glad, that is, until she heard Alex. She looked around to see what he meant. She saw the flower patterned kitchen curtains she loved, and the children's art taped up on the refrigerator door, some papers and books on the table to look through. "No way is this a mess. There are no dirty dishes in the sink, the pots on the stove are clean, the floor is clean. So there are some things on the kitchen table — so what? I just don't get it! The place looks lived in and that suits me fine!" Out of their differing comfort zones, Amy labels Alex a neatnik and Alex believes Amy is a clutterer.

"Planning Ahead" and "We'll Get There"
Beth was the kind of person who liked to plan ahead, especially where money was concerned. When she did the bill paying, she was careful to pay them well before the due date, and if at all possible to work things out so that as little as possible interest would have to be paid. She got frustrated when Bill took his turn and waited until the last minute to get at the bills, and became very uncomfortable if bills were paid late. She had learned to start reminding him early in the month that it was his turn to take care of the bills. But at the moment her concern was getting the two of them on a budget, so that they could start doing some work on the house. The bathroom had no shower and they were expecting their first child in just four months. Beth had told Bill that she would really like to have the shower installed by the time the baby was born. He had agreed that that was a good idea, but then had done absolutely nothing. All of her suggestions about calling around to get the best price, putting aside a part of the evening or certainly the weekend, seemed to accomplish nothing. Bill would simply respond, "I'll get to it," or "I'm tired tonight," or "Today was busy." Two months had gone by since they first talked about it, and Bill had promised to do some of the work himself to try to save money. Out of their differing comfort zones, Bill thinks Beth is nagging and Beth thinks Bill is a procrastinator.

"Leave Me Alone" and "Pamper Me"

By Friday, the flu had hit Carol with full force. She'd been fighting something all week and was relieved that at least tomorrow was Saturday and Charles could be home to take of her and the baby. She couldn't remember when she had felt this miserable before. Her head hurt; she felt like she was burning up. She felt so weak and shaky, she could hardly make it out of bed to the bathroom. She had asked Charles to bring up some crushed ice and some Coke syrup, so that she could take sips every now and then to soothe her cracked lips. She'd slept some, and when she woke up she thought the house was awfully quiet. She called for Charles, but he didn't seem to hear her. Getting out of bed, she saw the note taped to the door, "Will be back after dinner — the baby and I are over at my mom's, so you can rest undisturbed. See you later!" Carol was surprised and crestfallen as she thought, "So much for 'in sickness and in health.' So much for taking care of me. If he were sick, I'd be checking on him every twenty minutes or so, seeing if he wanted anything, if there is anything I could do to make him feel better." When Charles came home, it was his turn to be surprised. "I thought I was helping. If I were sick, I wouldn't want you fussing over me like that. I'd want to be left alone. Just close the door, and give me some peace and quiet. I'll let you know if I need anything." Out of their differing comfort zones, Carol thinks Charles has been heartless and Charles thinks Carol is acting like a bit of a baby.

Illusions Of Security

So far we've said that we've all learned ways of coping with the insecurities of life, with the fact that many things are out of our control, and with our fears of being small, weak, and alone. Part of being human means that we are imperfect people, we live in an imperfect world, and we are often driven by fears. We learn to make ourselves feel better about our frailties, vulnerabilities, and worries by finding some places where we do have some control and by gaining support from, through, and with other people.

And we keep striving for more — more certainty, more control, and more protection against vulnerability. We keep seeking — if only we were successful enough, had enough money or social status, if only we looked good enough, or were smart enough because we've convinced ourselves that when we arrive at the "enough," our vulnerability will be overcome.

These yearnings do not disappear after marriage, even though the promises you make to each other to share in joys and sorrows, good times and difficult ones, provide a solid base of trust and commitment for your relationship's life.

Longings for security still haunt married people, even tempting us to invest our hopes and energies in what we eventually realize is an illusion of security. No matter how successful our careers, no matter how rich, beautiful, knowledgeable, or even good we become, it never seems enough. Even when we've achieved one measure of security, another insecurity appears: "Now that we *have* money, how will we keep it? What it the best way for us to use it?" One of the challenges, then, in marriage is to think together about security values, goals, and investments.

The Bible has a lot to say about these human longings for security, especially on the subject of false security. Even in ancient times, it seems, people struggled with the same anxieties and longings that we do today. Many biblical stories describe these searchings and false leads. The prodigal son hoped for something more in the opportunities in a foreign land (Luke 15:11-32); the rich fool hoped his storehouses would provide security (Luke 12:13-21); the Pharisees put their hopes for security in perfect obedience to the law. These examples and many more are used to make the point that only God can give us absolute security. Only God is constantly faithful, loving, and forgiving. Only God is our "rock," the One who, in every moment, is reliable and trustworthy, even when our worlds, our relationships, our lives seem filled with anxiety.

Christian thoughts about security can be summarized in the prayer of Saint Augustine who lived in the fifth century. "You have made us for yourself, O God, and our hearts are restless still, until they rest in you." Augustine himself spent many years searching for love, for truth, and for peace before he came to this place of belief and trust in God.

The good news proclaimed in the Bible and among Christians is that God, who created us, claims us as daughters and sons and promises us the gift of companionship and relationship with God. This promise and claim is our secure treasure. Life in God's company means eating at Jesus' table, being nourished and fed by him, being transformed into more compassionate human beings and into the likeness of Christ. Life in God's company means gathering with other Christians to tell the story of Jesus dying and rising, to break the bread and celebrate life's victory over death. Living in the security of God's company gives us the strength to cope with the uncertainty and vulnerability of human life — and to take the risk of entering into and building up open, trust-filled, and committed marriages.

Summary

Your marriage relationship is intended to be a safe space where each of you can admit to vulnerability and offer encouragement and support to each other. Life's anxieties may make it difficult to remember this at times and to act toward each other in trust and good faith. It is helpful to understand each other's thinking about security, feelings of insecurity, and anxious patterns of behavior, so that you can better keep the promises which bind you together as wife and husband.

Our searchings for security point us to the God by whose love we are ultimately fed and sheltered.

Prayer Exercise 4: Prayer can be giving thanks for God, our rock and treasure. Read slowly together these ancient words in the Gospel of Luke. Even though they were written long ago, do they have any meanings for you and your relationship?

Jesus said to his disciples, "Therefore I tell you, do not worry about your life, what you will eat, or about your body, what you will wear. For life is more than food, and the body more than clothing.

"Consider the ravens: they neither sow nor reap, they have neither storehouse nor barn, and yet God feeds them. Of how much more value are you than the birds!

"And can any of you by worrying add a single hour to your span of life? If then you are not able to do so small a thing as that, why do you worry about the rest?

"Consider the lilies, how they grow: they neither toil nor spin yet I tell you, even Solomon in all his glory was not clothed like one of these. But if God so clothes the grass of the field, which is

alive today and tomorrow is thrown into the oven, how much more will he clothe you — you of little faith!

"And do not keep striving for what you are to eat and what you are to drink, and do not keep worrying. For it is the nations of the world that strive after all these things, and your Father knows that you need them. Instead, strive for his kingdom, and these things will be given to you as well.

"Do not be afraid, little flock, for it is your Father's good pleasure to give you the kingdom. Sell your possessions, and give alms. Make purses for yourselves that do not wear out, an unfailing treasure in heaven, where no thief comes near and no moth destroys. For where your treasure is, there your heart will be also."   — Luke 12:22-34

---

1. Human Sexuality — *ELCA Social Statement Working Draft*, p. 14.

2. Ronald Richardson, *Creating a Healthier Church*, Fortress Press, 1996, p. 66.

Chapter 6
Freedom/Responsibility —
The Gift Of Responsible Choice,
The Burden Of Self-preoccupation

Freedom is a cherished treasure. Political wars are fought in its name, teenagers protest for it, and numerous songs have been sung about it — from the egoistic song with the line, "I'll do it my way," to the civil rights hymn, "Lift every voice and sing till earth and heaven ring, ring with the harmonies of liberty." Freedom is an important theme in the Christian life. God creates us to be in communion with neighbor and with Godself, but our relationships with others and God are meant to be chosen freely and not coerced.

Each of us is faced with the decision about how we shall live. No one can answer for us.

Freedom involves wishing, valuing, and choosing. It's about exercising the right to speak from your heart's integrity and to express your individuality. As unique creatures of God, our choices should be freely made and therefore reveal our values, gifts, and specialness. As we make choices within the context of what is happening around us and to us, we influence the kind of person we are growing into. This "becoming" is a lifetime process shaped by our choices, our decisions, and our commitments.

Choosing to marry means committing yourself as much to the welfare of your partner as you are committed to your own well-being. You care about the partner's growth and becoming as you do your own. Choosing to live in marriage involves many joint decisions, taking into account each partner's uniqueness and the values, hopes, and actions that express that specialness. At their best, these joint decisions help to bring out and utilize each partner's capabilities and talents. Just as people often choose an occupation on the basis of their particular skills and talents, spouses can learn to think about each other's capabilities and interests when they make significant decisions. In the chapter on power, Sue was so absorbed in her own possibilities for professional growth, that in accepting her promotion she failed to take into account Rick's talents, interests, and growth.

Using your freedom responsibly to make choices involves considering the feelings, expectations, and hopes of other people and weighing the consequences of your decisions. How will your plans and actions affect your partner? Imagine what it would be like to walk in his or her shoes. For example, if your co-worker invites you to play volleyball, you find out how this invitation might affect your partner before you respond. Choosing freely and responsibly means learning to say, "Thanks for the invitation. Let me get back to you on that." It means making room for your partner's wishes and values.

FREEDOM

Being one's free and responsible self

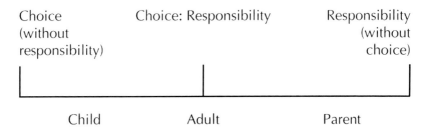

Choice (without responsibility)	Choice: Responsibility	Responsibility (without choice)
Child	Adult	Parent

The continuum above shows the misuse of freedom and the burden of responsibility at each end, and the gift of responsible choosing in the center.

On the left side is the misuse of freedom rooted in the attitude of entitlement which ignores the other person's wants and rights — "I am more special than you, therefore what I want counts more." Or it may be rooted in impatience and impulsiveness — "I can't stand the frustration of not having what I want when I want it." These attitudes may well be appropriate to some stages of child development, but when they carry over into adulthood, the impact on relationships is disastrous. A partner's absorbing self-interest and lack of empathy simply get in the way of making and keeping commitments. This blocks the couple's development of a loving and just marriage relationship.

On the right side is a misunderstanding of responsibility, which is rooted in the dread of making a mistake or not doing things perfectly.

This worry is so great that the gift of freedom cannot be experienced. Choices and decisions become an agonizing chore, and people on this end of the continuum feel personally responsible and accountable for things they have no real control over. An example of this would be a wife who feels guiltily responsible for her husband's social shyness or for her children's lack of musical talent.

Moving in from the ends of the continuum are the "parent" and "child" patterns of combining responsibility and freedom. A partner who may think and act responsibly at work and in other relationships may find himself or herself exercising less responsibility in the marital relationship, developing a parent-child relationship with the spouse.

This happens a bit with Melissa and Mark when it comes to getting jobs done together. Melissa likes to get the work done and then be free to relax, so she uses lots of organizational helps and schedules. Mark has learned a more relaxed approach. If something doesn't get taken care of today, it will be there tomorrow.

It was important to Melissa that she and Mark be equally involved in the thinking and planning of their wedding. Mark agreed but soon began secretly to feel overwhelmed by Melissa's organizational style. Her preference was for them to set out a time line representing the six months prior to the date of their wedding and then to assign tasks to be done by specific dates. When Mark inadvertently missed the first two deadlines, Melissa became anxious about how everything would get accomplished if they did not stay on the schedule as planned. She began to check and remind Mark, on a very frequent basis, suspecting that if she didn't "keep after him" things wouldn't happen. Mark found himself resisting the reminders and began to drag his feet even more. He teasingly called her "the drill sergeant" and told her to lighten up, not to make the wedding such a chore. "I'll get it done, maybe not until the day before the wedding, but it'll get done."

But Melissa simply stepped up her efforts to goad and even shame him into action. "Am I going to have to take care of EVERYTHING? Couldn't you manage to do just one thing a day? Is that too much to ask? I don't think so!" The more she took on a *parental* tone in stressing Mark's responsibility, the more he slipped into a *child-like resistance*. As you might have guessed, the more child-like resistance on Mark's part, the stronger became Melissa's parental response.

For each, this particular situation brought out values and even feelings associated with their family of origin dynamics, without either one realizing it. Melissa, as the eldest child in a family who held strongly to the value of cooperation, had been given many responsibilities for the care of her siblings and for the household. She learned to think in terms of division of duties and supervising her younger sisters in their responsibilities, and to take satisfaction in these capabilities. But Mark, the youngest in the family, was used to being left pretty much on his own, especially after his mother died. Even while she was alive, Mark was not expected to do things like make his bed, help with dishes, cleaning, and the like. There were some arguments with his brother James about who should do what, when James would try to "boss" him around, but Mark developed his own timetable and his own ways of doing things.

Once Melissa and Mark can identify that their present struggle is related to their family of origin experiences, they can move away from such parent-child interactions and think about how to work better together.

When couples, for the most part, are able to stay within the middle range of the continuum and exercise freedom responsibly with one another, there are opportunities for the relationship to grow and be enriched. There are certain important freedoms to express: first, openness to the other's uniqueness, and second, affirmation and appreciation of each other and their relationship.

You Are Uniquely Made, Uniquely Gifted

This may seem obvious, but it still bears saying: Each of you is unique, even though you may share with one another many, many common tastes, feelings, thoughts, values, and experiences. Still, each of you sees the world differently in some ways and you express yourselves differently. This "differentness" was probably part of your fascination and attraction to each other. But the differentness can be frustrating at times, too, when you'd really prefer that your partner be more like you in the ways you do things or think about things. For example, Jenny loves John's steadiness and calmness; "He is my anchor in life!" she says appreciatively. But at times when he seems to drag his feet on some new proposal of hers, she complains in frustration, "He is such a stick-in-the-mud, so closed to change!" without seeing that these experiences of John are really two sides of the same coin.

- Take time now to reflect about yourselves in terms of your uniqueness. Think about your families of origin, your personalities, your tastes, preferences, your attitudes and values about money, children, work, church, religion, recreation, friendship, your ways of showing affection, appreciation, anger, etc.

- What similarities do you notice between you?

- In what ways do you think these similarities are good for your relationship? Are there ways in which these are not so good? Why?

- What differences (differentness) do you notice between you?

- In what ways do you think these are good for your relationship? Are there ways in which these are not so good? Why?

- Can you see any places where these personal differences are two sides of the same coin?

Affirmation And Appreciation Of Each Other

One of the sad things that can happen in marriages and families is that people don't think to express appreciation and affirmation of each other. They may even be embarrassed by tender and warm feelings, so their habit is to speak only to give complaint. When one wife grumbled to her husband that he never complimented her on anything, he replied, "I'll let you know if there's something I don't like. If you don't hear from me it means you are doing okay." This viewpoint badly misses out on the joy in affirming and celebrating the gifts partners bring to each other. Taking these riches for granted leads to a tired emotional flatness and a loss of important nourishment for the relationship.

Take some time now to think about your own relationship by completing the following sentences:

- I feel appreciated as a unique person, loved, important and valued by my partner when ...

- I feel less appreciated or even taken for granted and unimportant, when my partner ...

- I show my partner I appreciate, love, and value him/her when ...

- The way I can tell that my partner feels unappreciated or unimportant is that he/she ...

- I would like my spouse to do this more often (e.g., express his/her feelings about me/our relationship; affirm something I do; say "thank you," etc.) ...

- I would like to show my partner I appreciate him/her more often by ...

  Now take time to exchange and talk over your responses with each other.

Managing Differentness

Although the two of you share a common commitment to the marriage relationship, you are two unique persons whose personal values, tastes, and preferences will inevitably present conflicts of agenda and interest. These different preferences may be small, e.g., methods for doing the laundry, cleaning, or mowing the lawn. They may be larger and more significant differences in values, e.g. having to do with the importance of education, work, religion, or money. Any of these may be personal differences in values and preferences that you already know about and are ready for, or they may seem to come out of nowhere and surprise you both. In any case it helps to be able to identify the issues of differentness at hand and learn to approach them using all the skills of communication, negotiation, and conflict management that have been mentioned in previous chapters.

If we can talk about the freedoms in relationship as being open to your partner's uniqueness, and being able to appreciate each other and your relationship, then we should also mention some "unfreedoms." These are attitudes and behaviors that tie your relationship in knots. In a recent study on why marriages fail,[1] these un-freeing attitudes and behaviors were named "the four horsemen of the apocalypse":

Defensiveness, that is denying responsibility, making excuses, and cross-complaining instead of listening to the partner's concern and trying to learn how s/he is experiencing you. A husband complains that the wife has not put away things she borrowed, and she responds, "Big deal, at least I'm on time, which is more than I can say for you half the time."

Criticizing someone's entire personality or character, rather than the specific behavior which bothers you. "You are a slob" instead of "I don't like it when you leave your towel lying on the floor."

Contempt. Here the intent is to insult the partner. "You are really stupid, incredibly inept. No wonder you can't get a job. Who would want to pay such a moron?" The insulter goes for the jugular vein, aiming the abuse right at the partner's sense of self-worth. Sometimes this takes the form of hostile humor, sneering, and mocking.

Stonewalling. This is a refusal to engage the partner, shutting him or her out as though s/he hasn't said anything worth the effort of communicating about. In response to a wife's complaint, for example, a husband may say in a sarcastic way, "Whatever you say," or he may simply keep a stony silence.

These unfreedoms need not mean the end of a relationship, but they do serve as danger signals. Therefore couples need to remember or learn how to complain in helpful ways. It is better to express anger, disappointment, and disagreement in clear, short, civil, and specific ways, than it is to suppress the complaint. One of the most powerful tools for healing your relationship is letting your partner know that you want to understand him or her as a valued person who is unique, distinct from you. Instead of attacking or negating your differentness, let your partner know that you are open to hearing and considering his or her view and that you are committed to finding ways to honor having your two unique personalities in your marriage. This helps you to keep valuing and choosing each other, and thereby to live out your promises to join with one another.

The Freedom Of Forgiveness

When partners do get caught in self-preoccupation and the unfreedoms of defensiveness, criticizing, contempt, and stonewalling, it is often due to an underlying spirit of resentful blaming when a partner resents the other's shortcoming, mistake, or hurtful act. For

example, Sue is understandably annoyed at her husband John for flirt-
ing with another woman at a recent party. One response to this annoyance is for her to speak to him simply and directly: "Seeing you
spend so much time alone with Martha at the party really bothered
me. What am I, chopped liver, that you preferred to laugh and joke
with her and totally ignore me? What was going on with you?" Ideally this will lead to a mutual process of sorting out perceptions, feelings, and intentions, and to the possibility of restoring good will in
the relationship.

If, however, Sue mulls over John's behavior by fanning it with the
spirit of self-righteous and resentful blame, she will find it difficult
even to think about forgiving John's offense to her: "How could he
even think of behaving in such a *hateful* way? It is unacceptable for
him to do such a wrong and hurtful thing! *I would never* do that to him!
He should be *punished* for hurting and embarrassing me in front of our
friends. If he really loved me, he would never have treated me in such
a way. He's a cad and I'll never be able to trust him fully again." Her
spirit of self-righteousness leads her to think about John's wrongness
in contrast to her own goodness, and away from the thoughts about
forgiveness and hopes for reconciliation between them.

John Patton in his book *Is Human Forgiveness Possible?* makes a
powerful statement about what is involved in forgiving:

> *Human forgiveness is not doing something, but discovering
> something — that I am more like those who have hurt me
> than different from them. I am able to forgive when I dis-
> cover that I am in no position to forgive.*[2]

This means that couples need to be alert (as do we all) to how they
find themselves reacting to feelings of disappointment, hurt, and be-
trayal of trust that inevitably emerge as two unique partners live out
their lives together. It means paying special attention to judgments they
are making about each other in response to being hurt or disappointed.
In such situations it may be tempting to blame and demonize the other,
while sanctifying ourselves. But instead of dwelling on blame, revenge,
and bitterness, these are good times to be honest with ourselves about
our own fallibility and need for forgiveness.

We often make the mistake of equating the work of forgiving with forgetting, expecting that the true sign of forgiveness is to have erased all memory of the offense. Actually, forgiving is more a process of re-interpreting, re-seeing, enlarging our perspective. We don't so much forget, as we remember the meaning of the event differently. Especially at these times it is important to remember that we ourselves daily receive the gift of God's forgiving and accepting love. We don't deserve it, we don't earn it, and the further miracle is that in being so abundantly graced, we are freed to let go of our resentments and be loving ourselves.

Re-choosing For Commitment

Affirming and appreciating each other, learning to love and value the other for the imperfect person he or she is, being willing to accept faults and forgive hurts and disappointments that inevitably happen as a result of being human — these are all important ways of investing in each other and in the marriage relationship. In these ways partners keep re-choosing their marriage.

Commitment to marriage, then, is a life-long process, acted out in everyday activities. It is expressed when one of you gets out of bed grumpy in the morning, when you make decisions about how money is spent, what you plan to do on any given day, and how you share the grunt work of daily living. Commitment is acted out in the middle of quarrels by refusing to give up on working it out together. As Elizabeth Achtemeier puts it:

> *In all life's seasons, and in all life's moods, we decide for or against our marriage, not only by what we think and feel but by what we do.*[3]

At times for some, the feeling of "being in love" seems to fade or even disappear. This may be alarming to the one who is experiencing this kind of dry spell. Comparing the earlier sense of thrill and elation, s/he may mourn in despair that the marriage is dead, over. S/he may even conclude that to go on in the marriage would be to live a lie.

Actually, these viewpoints are flawed. The identifying mark of love is not really "walking two feet off the ground," although certainly feelings of excitement and well-being may be a part of loving and feeling loved in return. Even so, loving and "falling-in-love" are not the same thing. Falling-in-love is largely a "feeling" experience, a deliciously hopeless infatuation, where one feels helplessly drawn to the romance of it all. Mature love, though, is not simply a feeling experience; it is a thinking and acting one as well. It involves a way of "being-with" one's partner. Feelings are sometimes fickle and we may not have much control over how we feel at any given day or hour. We do have choices, though, about how we act toward our partner. Despite how we feel, we can choose to act in caring ways and to follow through on our promises and commitments to life-long faithfulness.

This means that when a partner reports "falling-out-of-love," the change in feeling is very much related to whatever else has been going on in his or her relationship world. The loss of romantic love does not usually "just happen" but more likely is a result of self-preoccupation and personal insecurity that play themselves out in patterns of unrealistic expectation and marital neglect. "Falling-out-of-love" is very much connected to partners' day-to-day behavior with each other.

If you should find yourselves in this situation, it may help for the two of you to talk about these feelings, experiences, and issues with your pastor. The remarkable thing is that when couples re-choose the relationship by paying attention to each other again, when they choose to act with each other in caring ways, they may rekindle the relationship's warmth and begin to experience themselves once again as loving partners. The point is that instead of holding back and simply hoping for feelings of passion to return, partners can begin, even in the absence of romantic feelings, to act lovingly on their commitment to the partner's welfare and to the marital promises that they made to each other. To undergird these efforts, what is needed on the part of Christian married partners is an awareness of God's lively action in our lives. What is needed is to remind ourselves that God has a purpose for each of our lives; God is working in us and through us to fulfill those purposes.

Marriage has been described as a "workshop for love" in the sense that over and over again couples find themselves asking and responding to life's question, "How do I/we love in *this* situation?" Christians believe that God's presence and blessing are always available to help in making responsible and loving choices and in fulfilling commitments. Empowered by this sense of being connected to God's loving purposes, marital partners try to honor each other's uniqueness, affirm each other's gifts, and appreciate their life-long becoming. They keep renewing their commitments to the well-being of the partner and the relationship. Together, they choose to live out their faith understandings with each other.

> **Prayer Exercise 5:** Prayer can be giving thanks that God does not leave us alone in our times of self-preoccupation, for God's presence is always with us if we will notice it. We express thanks that God sent Jesus to live among us, to show us God's abundant love, and to invite us to say yes to life with God. When we choose God we become the human beings we are meant to be. We are freed from our self-absorption to live gratefully, graciously, and lovingly toward God and other people.

Read together the well-known words of Martin Luther on the freedom of a Christian:

> *A Christian is the most free lord of all and subject to none; a Christian is the most dutiful servant of all and subject to everyone.*
>
> *Hence as our heavenly Father has in Christ freely come to our aid, we also ought freely to help our neighbor through our body and its works, and each one should become as it were a Christ to the other that we may be Christs to one another and Christ may be the same in all, that is that we may be truly Christians.*
>
> *Your faith is sufficient for you, through which God has given you all things. See, according to this rule the good things we have from God should flow from one to the other and be common to all, so that everyone should "put on" their neighbor and so conduct themselves as if they were in the other's place ... By faith Christians are caught up beyond themselves into God. By Love they descend beneath themselves into their neighbors.*[4]

Even though the language of servant and lord belong to a different time and place, do these remarks about Christian freedom have any meaning for you and your relationship? How are you/can you be a Christ to your partner? How is/can your partner be a Christ to you?

1. Gottman, John, *Why Marriages Succeed or Fail*, Simon and Schuster, 1994.

2. Patton, John, *Is Human Forgiveness Possible?* Abingdon, 1987.

3. Achtemeier, Elizabeth, *The Committed Marriage*, Westminster Press, 1976.

4. Luther, Martin, "The Freedom of a Christian," *Martin Luther's Basic Theological Writings*, edited by Timothy Lull, Fortress Press, 1989.

Bride's Workbook

Now Bring Your Joy To This Wedding

Couples In Premarital Preparation

Norma S. Wood

and

Lisa M. Leber

CSS Publishing Company, Inc., Lima, Ohio

Forming A New Family

Making A Genogram
(refer to handbook page 16)

Chart your family genogram in the space below.

Birth Order And Gender
(refer to pages 19-20)

Look at your patterns. Are both of you comfortable? Does anyone feel a bit burdened or pushed? Where and how? How might you improve on this?

_____

_____

_____

_____

_____

_____

_____

_____

Now notice what were the roles of males and females in your families as you were growing up. Some families have a strict code of behavior, e.g., females do all the "inside-the-house" work, and males do all the "outside-the-house" work, while others make few distinctions, i.e., males do their share of cooking and cleaning and females take their turns at yard, car, and basement care.

What difference did it make in your family that you were male or female? How are you now thinking about the division of responsibility in your relationship? Is gender a major factor here, or not?

_____

_____

_____

_____

_____

_____

_____

Change And Loss: The Influence Of Life Events
(refer to pages 20-22)

Now go to your own genogram again and think about what major changes have happened in your family's history and life over the last twenty years, for example. You've already recorded dates of births, marriages, deaths, and divorces. Now think about other changes, geographic moves, major illnesses or disabilities, job changes, etc. List these in the right hand corner of your genogram along with their dates.

Now think about how your family reacted to these. What do you notice? When people are upset, do they reach out to other family members, or do they pretty much handle things on their own?

_____

_____

_____

_____

_____

Think about one loss event, such as a death or separation. Did members express their feelings liberally and loudly or were they more private and contained about their feelings?

_____

_____

_____

_____

Do the same thing with an event of celebration, such as a big achievement or a birth or even the announcement of your own marriage. How would you describe your family's way of responding?

_____

_____

_____

_____

We'll be looking further into family reactive patterns in each of the next chapters. For now, share your noticings and discoveries with each other. If there are any observations that you think might be helpful to understanding your own relationship, mention these to each other for further consideration and reflection.

Family Values
(refer to pages 22-24)

Think about *education*. What was communicated to you about grades, subjects, programs, about learning in general? Was your schooling something your parents took more or less interest in? Perhaps there were rules in your family about when homework had to be done, or about grades and report cards. In Mark's family, for example, there was an unspoken rule that a college education was a must. Even though Mark had no idea of what he wanted to do after high school and wished he could take a year's break from schooling, he was expected to go on and get a college degree in something. In Melissa's family, this emphasis was missing, although they did not discourage Melissa's initiatives.

_____

_____

_____

_____

_____

_____

What about *work*? What are the occupations in your family? How did they view their work? As something that had to be done in order to make a living? A satisfaction? A combination?

_____

_____

_____

_____

_____

_____

What about work around the house? Who does what? What were your responsibilities? What rules ("Before you go out to play, watch television, read that book, I want you to ...") and incentives (allowance, privileges, praise, punishments, and penalties) did your parents use to motivate you to carry out these responsibilities?

_____

_____

_____

_____

_____

_____

What did you learn about the value of *money*? Were you encouraged to get a job to help pay for your own expenses? To help out the family? Did the family urge saving for a rainy day? What were the rules about paying cash or using credit cards?

_____

_____

_____

_____

_____

What about *religion*? Did your family practice a faith? Did you take part in a religious education program? What was communicated to you about religious days and holidays? How did your family regard Sundays, for example? What were the family traditions around Christmas? What are some of the values you hold as you plan for a meaningful wedding?

_____

_____

_____

_____

_____

Now, take time together to notice what are the similarities and differences in your families' values. Where are the two of you in relation to these values? The point of doing this — just to say it one more time — is that we tend to use our experiences in our families of origin to develop marital standards of what is right, wrong, and normal. By studying your families as cultures of influence, and noting the ways in which each of you is similar and different from your own family and from each other's, you are helping yourselves to form your own family unit. While sharing similarities tends to strengthen those values, differences are often challenging for couples to handle. For this reason it's important to recognize differences and begin to find ways to accept them or to collaborate to find solutions to the challenges your differences create. Noticing these areas of value similarity and difference is an important first step.

Similarities:

_____
_____
_____
_____
_____
_____

Differences:

_____
_____
_____
_____
_____
_____

Intimacy — The Gift Of Presence, The Burden Of Alienation

(refer to pages 29-32)

INTIMACY

Being Close, Knowing/Being Known

Individuality - - - - - - - - - - - - I/We - - - - - - - - - - - Togetherness

Using the continuum above to pay attention to some of your assumptions and expectations about intimacy, take some time to read the questions below, ponder them, jot down some notes, and then share your thinking with your partner.

What do you do to try to get close to your partner? How do you think your partner tries to get close to you?

_____

_____

_____

_____

_____

_____

What is going on when you do feel close? Are there certain conditions that you feel need to be there in order for you to want to be close? Do certain situations lead to your feelings of closeness? Try remembering where you were the last time you felt really close to one another.

_____

_____

_____

_____

_____

_____

What is going on when you don't feel close? Try remembering the last time you felt distant from your partner. What did it feel like? What did it mean to you?

_____

_____

_____

_____

_____

_____

_____

Are there times when you would like to understand your partner better or to be better understood? When are some of these?

_____

_____

_____

_____

_____

_____

How do you let your partner know when you wish some time to your-self rather than be together? How does he or she let you know? Do the two of you come right out and say so or do you use non-verbal ways of trying to convey this?

_____

_____

_____

_____

_____

_____

What did you learn about intimacy in your family culture? Do you see any connections between what you learned there and your expectations of each other?

_____

_____

_____

_____

_____

_____

Communication
(refer to pages 32-34)

Noticing what makes for poor communication can be quite helpful in discovering what makes it better. You and your partner might explore this by selecting a topic to talk about for five minutes, such as how you'll spend your first vacation, or what would be an ideal weekend. During this time, use three poor communication tactics. You might try things such as looking away from your partner, looking bored, interrupting, not listening to what was being said, not talking yourself, not responding to what your partner says, attending to something else, yawning, etc. All of these behaviors signal lack of interest and lack of desire to know and be connected to each other. After five minutes, stop and talk about what it was like for each of you to employ these tactics. Did you recognize the other's tactics? What did it feel like to be on the receiving end? What was most disturbing to you?

Now talk for five minutes on the same topic, but this time each of you use three communication strategies that you think will help you know and be connected to your partner. After five minutes, stop and again talk about what it was like.

Compare your set of clear communication ideas with the list of guidelines below.

— Look at your partner and notice facial expressions, body language, and tone of voice.

— Use listening, acknowledging responses.

— Listen fully to what is being said before responding. Don't think about your response while your partner is still talking.

— Be open to the other's point of view, suggestions.

— Use "I" statements and be as specific as you can be about what you think, feel, and want.

— Paraphrase what you've heard.

— Check out your perceptions. (Am I sensing that you are annoyed?)

— Ask open questions. (Can you tell me more about that?)

— Avoid leading questions. (You know I'm right, don't you?)

— Don't escalate your voice to make your point.

— Don't cut your partner off.

— Don't criticize or argue with her or his experience. (You shouldn't feel that way! or What a dumb thing to think!)

— Sit so that you can see your partner's face when you are talking together.

— Put down the newspaper or book you are reading. Turn off the television.

Empathy
(refer to pages 35-36)

Try to recall an experience when you really felt listened to, understood, and accepted for who you are. Tell your partner what this was like for you.

Try to think of a time when you had difficulty understanding what was going on with your partner. See if you can explore what might help you get into his or her shoes. Sometimes it helps a lot to try imagining what is was like to grow up in your partner's family culture because it makes clearer why certain values are important to him or her.

_____

_____

_____

_____

_____

_____

Power — The Gift Of Collaboration, The Burden Of Hoarding

(refer to pages 46-47)

Take some time to think about your family of origin, your decision-making process, and your expectations for how you and your spouse-to-be will work out the details of your life together.

How were decisions made in your family? Did your parents make the decisions about family matters on their own? Were the children involved in discussions about family matters like moving, vacations, how they would be disciplined, whether they would get an allowance, etc.? Did you have "family conferences" where important topics were discussed? Did Mom and Dad make decisions for you (and your siblings)?

_____

_____

_____

_____

_____

_____

_____

Was one parent the final authority figure for the family? Did your parents divide decision-making on the basis of traditional gender roles? (i.e., Did your father take care of the finances and your mother take care of day-to-day decisions?)

_____

_____

_____

_____

_____

_____

Did you see your parents disagree? Do you know how your parents
worked out differences of opinion? Did one parent defer to the other
when there was disagreement? Was it always the same parent, or did it
depend on the issue?

_____

_____

_____

_____

_____

_____

What kinds of decisions were you allowed to make for yourself? Were
you allowed to spend your money the way you wanted to? Choose
your own career or college? Were you given the power and freedom to
buy your own clothes or pick the extracurricular activities you wanted
to do?

_____

_____

_____

_____

_____

_____

What did you do when you disagreed with your parents about something? Were you given the opportunity to talk it out? Did your parents
have the final say?

_____

_____

_____

_____

_____

_____

How do you make decisions now? How do you and your spouse-to-be make decisions together? Does one of you make decisions about certain things, for example, what you do in your time together or what kind of wedding you'll have? What happens when you disagree about something? Does one of you defer to the other? Is one of you more likely than the other to want to talk things out? Does it depend on the issue?

_____

_____

_____

_____

_____

_____

Conflict
(refer to pages 47-51)

As an introduction to the collaborative process, take some time to work on the following conflict resolution exercise.

1. Select one or two conflicts the two of you have had in the past.

2. Try to determine whether this is a misunderstanding or a disagreement.

    Misunderstanding: "I thought you meant this, but discovered as we talked that you meant that" or "I just assumed when I heard you talking on the phone that you intended to ... but as we talked I realized that I had taken what you said out of context" or "When I saw you frowning at me, I thought you were angry with me and didn't know, until you told me later, that you had a headache."

    Disagreement: "I want to invite my mother to Thanksgiving dinner with us and you want us to eat alone" or "I want to relax after dinner with a newspaper and clean up later and you want to get the dishes done, the food put away as soon as we're done eating" (in other words, you understand each other very well, but disagree about an issue or area).

3. If your conflict was in fact a disagreement, at what step in the process toward negotiation and reconciliation did you stumble or get blocked?

4. Identify the issues of disagreement.

5. Decide on a time to discuss these.

6. Take turns hearing each person's perspective. What does each person want? Why?

7. Check that each has accurately heard the other's perspective.

8. Brainstorm about alternatives. (This is a time for creativity!)

9. Consider prayerfully what the two of you are discussing.

10. Make a decision and plans for future review and evaluation of your joint decision.

Power And Anger
(refer to page 54)

Anger Exercise: Take a few moments to answer the following questions. See how you deal with/react to anger and then talk about your answers with your partner.

1. What words or pictures come to mind when you try to describe anger?

2. How did your parents express their anger toward you and toward each other?

3. What conflict management styles did they tend to use? Avoiding, competing, accommodating, compromising, collaborating?

4. How did other members of your family deal with anger and conflict?

5. Describe what your feelings were when someone was angry with you.

6. How did your family react when you got angry?

7. How do you react when your partner is angry?

8. Do you respond any differently when s/he is angry with you?

9. How do you let your partner know that you are angry?

10. How do you let her/him know that you are "over" your anger?

11. Are there other feelings you associate with being angry?

12. How would you describe yourself? As slow or quick to anger? As one who holds a grudge or is quick to forgive and forget?

These questions are adapted from *Couples in Treatment: Techniques and Approaches for Effective Practice*, Gerald R. Weeks and Stephen Treat, Brunner/ Mazel, 1992.

Security — The Gift Of Commitment, The Burden Of Anxiety

(refer to pages 59-62)

SECURITY

Anxiety - - - - - - - - Relative Absence of Threat - - - - - - - - Anxiety
Fear of chaos   Fear of abandonment
Response is creating   Response is dependence on
good order   partner or security "stuff"

Using the continuum above and illustration on page 58 of the handbook to notice some of your ideas about security and your anxieties, read the questions below, jot down some notes about your observations, and then share your thinking with your partner. Perhaps as you talk together, you will better understand and cope with the expressions of security and anxiety in your relationship.

What did you learn about security in your family culture? (You can get at this question, too, by thinking about your family's biggest worry.)

_____

_____

_____

_____

_____

Do you see any connections between what you learned there and your expectations of your partner?

_____

_____

_____

_____

_____

Were there any "events" in the life of your family similar to the death
of Mark's mother or Melissa's aunt's divorce and move away? How
did these affect you?

_____
_____
_____
_____
_____
_____
_____

How did you know when members of your family were worried?
Did they tell you or did you notice certain changes in the way they
behaved?

_____
_____
_____
_____
_____
_____

What do you think you worry about most?

_____
_____
_____
_____
_____
_____

What do you do about it to try to make yourself feel calmer and less anxious?

_____

_____

_____

_____

_____

_____

Is there something, someone, some activity you think might operate as your "security blanket"?

_____

_____

_____

_____

_____

_____

What do you think your partner worries most about?

_____

_____

_____

_____

_____

How do you know when she/he is anxious and worried?

_____

_____

_____

_____

_____

How do you try to make things safe again with each other?

_____

_____

_____

_____

_____

_____

Do you see any similarities between the two of you in the ways you manage anxiety? Do you see any differences?

_____

_____

_____

_____

_____

_____

Thinking about your responses to the questions above, identify at least two things you think might be key to maintaining trust and stability in your relationship.

_____

_____

_____

_____

_____

_____

Marital Comfort Zones

Reread the three scenarios on pages 63-65 of the handbook, each one describing a common relationship situation in which individual comfort zones are jostled. See if you find yourself identifying with any of these situations, then share your reactions with your partner.

Freedom/Responsibility —
The Gift Of Responsible Choice,
The Burden Of Self-preoccupation

You Are Uniquely Made, Uniquely Gifted
(refer to pages 72-73)

Take time now to reflect about yourselves in terms of your uniqueness. Think about your families of origin, your personalities, your tastes, preferences, your attitudes and values about money, children, work, church, religion, recreation, friendship, your ways of showing affection, appreciation, anger, etc.

What similarities do you notice between you?

_____

_____

_____

_____

_____

_____

_____

_____

In what ways do you think these similarities are good for your relationship? Are there ways in which these are not so good? Why?

_____

_____

_____

_____

_____

_____

_____

_____

What differences (differentness) do you notice between you?

_____

_____

_____

_____

_____

_____

_____

_____

In what ways do you think these are good for your relationship? Are there ways in which these are not so good? Why?

_____

_____

_____

_____

_____

_____

_____

Can you see any places where these personal differences are two sides of the same coin?

_____

_____

_____

_____

_____

_____

_____

_____

Affirmation And Appreciation Of Each Other
(refer to pages 73-74)

Take some time now to think about your own relationship by completing the following sentences:

I feel appreciated as a unique person, loved, important, and valued by my partner when ...

_____

_____

_____

_____

_____

_____

I feel less appreciated or even taken for granted and unimportant when my partner ...

_____

_____

_____

_____

_____

_____

I show my partner I appreciate, love, and value him/her when ...

_____

_____

_____

_____

_____

_____

The way I can tell that my partner feels unappreciated or unimportant is that he/she ...

_____

_____

_____

_____

_____

_____

I would like my spouse to do this more often (e.g., express his/her feelings about me/our relationship; affirm something I do; say "thank you," etc.) ...

_____

_____

_____

_____

_____

_____

I would like to show my partner I appreciate him/her more often by ...

_____

_____

_____

_____

_____

_____

Now take time to exchange and talk over your responses with each other.

Groom's Workbook

Now Bring Your Joy To This Wedding

Couples In Premarital Preparation

Norma S. Wood

and

Lisa M. Leber

CSS Publishing Company, Inc., Lima, Ohio

Forming A New Family

Making A Genogram
(refer to handbook page 16)

Chart your family genogram in the space below.

Birth Order And Gender
(refer to pages 19-20)

Look at your patterns. Are both of you comfortable? Does anyone feel a bit burdened or pushed? Where and how? How might you improve on this?

_____

_____

_____

_____

_____

_____

_____

_____

_____

Now notice what were the roles of males and females in your families as you were growing up. Some families have a strict code of behavior, e.g., females do all the "inside-the-house" work, and males do all the "outside-the-house" work, while others make few distinctions, i.e., males do their share of cooking and cleaning and females take their turns at yard, car, and basement care.

What difference did it make in your family that you were male or female? How are you now thinking about the division of responsibility in your relationship? Is gender a major factor here, or not?

_____

_____

_____

_____

_____

_____

_____

_____

Change And Loss: The Influence Of Life Events
(refer to pages 20-22)

Now go to your own genogram again and think about what major changes have happened in your family's history and life over the last twenty years, for example. You've already recorded dates of births, marriages, deaths, and divorces. Now think about other changes, geographic moves, major illnesses or disabilities, job changes, etc. List these in the right hand corner of your genogram along with their dates.

Now think about how your family reacted to these. What do you notice? When people are upset, do they reach out to other family members, or do they pretty much handle things on their own?

_____

_____

_____

_____

_____

Think about one loss event, such as a death or separation. Did members express their feelings liberally and loudly or were they more private and contained about their feelings?

_____

_____

_____

_____

Do the same thing with an event of celebration, such as a big achievement or a birth or even the announcement of your own marriage. How would you describe your family's way of responding?

_____

_____

_____

_____

We'll be looking further into family reactive patterns in each of the next chapters. For now, share your noticings and discoveries with each other. If there are any observations that you think might be helpful to understanding your own relationship, mention these to each other for further consideration and reflection.

Family Values
(refer to pages 22-24)

Think about *education*. What was communicated to you about grades, subjects, programs, about learning in general? Was your schooling something your parents took more or less interest in? Perhaps there were rules in your family about when homework had to be done, or about grades and report cards. In Mark's family, for example, there was an unspoken rule that a college education was a must. Even though Mark had no idea of what he wanted to do after high school and wished he could take a year's break from schooling, he was expected to go on and get a college degree in something. In Melissa's family, this emphasis was missing, although they did not discourage Melissa's initiatives.

_____

_____

_____

_____

_____

_____

What about *work*? What are the occupations in your family? How did they view their work? As something that had to be done in order to make a living? A satisfaction? A combination?

_____

_____

_____

_____

_____

_____

What about work around the house? Who does what? What were your responsibilities? What rules ("Before you go out to play, watch television, read that book, I want you to ...") and incentives (allowance, privileges, praise, punishments, and penalties) did your parents use to motivate you to carry out these responsibilities?

_____

_____

_____

_____

_____

_____

What did you learn about the value of *money*? Were you encouraged to get a job to help pay for your own expenses? To help out the family? Did the family urge saving for a rainy day? What were the rules about paying cash or using credit cards?

_____

_____

_____

_____

_____

What about *religion*? Did your family practice a faith? Did you take part in a religious education program? What was communicated to you about religious days and holidays? How did your family regard Sundays, for example? What were the family traditions around Christmas? What are some of the values you hold as you plan for a meaningful wedding?

_____

_____

_____

_____

_____

Now, take time together to notice what are the similarities and differences in your families' values. Where are the two of you in relation to these values? The point of doing this — just to say it one more time — is that we tend to use our experiences in our families of origin to develop marital standards of what is right, wrong, and normal. By studying your families as cultures of influence, and noting the ways in which each of you is similar and different from your own family and from each other's, you are helping yourselves to form your own family unit. While sharing similarities tends to strengthen those values, differences are often challenging for couples to handle. For this reason it's important to recognize differences and begin to find ways to accept them or to collaborate to find solutions to the challenges your differences create. Noticing these areas of value similarity and difference is an important first step.

Similarities:

_____

_____

_____

_____

_____

_____

Differences:

_____

_____

_____

_____

_____

_____

Intimacy — The Gift Of Presence, The Burden Of Alienation

(refer to pages 29-32)

INTIMACY

Being Close, Knowing/Being Known
Individuality - - - - - - - - - - - - I/We - - - - - - - - - - - Togetherness

Using the continuum above to pay attention to some of your assumptions and expectations about intimacy, take some time to read the questions below, ponder them, jot down some notes, and then share your thinking with your partner.

What do you do to try to get close to your partner? How do you think your partner tries to get close to you?

_____

_____

_____

_____

_____

_____

What is going on when you do feel close? Are there certain conditions that you feel need to be there in order for you to want to be close? Do certain situations lead to your feelings of closeness? Try remembering where you were the last time you felt really close to one another.

_____

_____

_____

_____

_____

_____

What is going on when you don't feel close? Try remembering the last time you felt distant from your partner. What did it feel like? What did it mean to you?

_____

_____

_____

_____

_____

_____

_____

Are there times when you would like to understand your partner better or to be better understood? When are some of these?

_____

_____

_____

_____

_____

_____

_____

How do you let your partner know when you wish some time to yourself rather than be together? How does he or she let you know? Do the two of you come right out and say so or do you use non-verbal ways of trying to convey this?

_____

_____

_____

_____

_____

_____

_____

What did you learn about intimacy in your family culture? Do you see any connections between what you learned there and your expectations of each other?

_____

_____

_____

_____

_____

_____

Communication
(refer to pages 32-34)

Noticing what makes for poor communication can be quite helpful in discovering what makes it better. You and your partner might explore this by selecting a topic to talk about for five minutes, such as how you'll spend your first vacation, or what would be an ideal weekend. During this time, use three poor communication tactics. You might try things such as looking away from your partner, looking bored, interrupting, not listening to what was being said, not talking yourself, not responding to what your partner says, attending to something else, yawning, etc. All of these behaviors signal lack of interest and lack of desire to know and be connected to each other. After five minutes, stop and talk about what it was like for each of you to employ these tactics. Did you recognize the other's tactics? What did it feel like to be on the receiving end? What was most disturbing to you?

Now talk for five minutes on the same topic, but this time each of you use three communication strategies that you think will help you know and be connected to your partner. After five minutes, stop and again talk about what it was like.

Compare your set of clear communication ideas with the list of guidelines below.

— Look at your partner and notice facial expressions, body language, and tone of voice.

— Use listening, acknowledging responses.

— Listen fully to what is being said before responding. Don't think about your response while your partner is still talking.

— Be open to the other's point of view, suggestions.

— Use "I" statements and be as specific as you can be about what you think, feel, and want.

— Paraphrase what you've heard.

— Check out your perceptions. (Am I sensing that you are annoyed?)

— Ask open questions. (Can you tell me more about that?)

— Avoid leading questions. (You know I'm right, don't you?)

— Don't escalate your voice to make your point.

— Don't cut your partner off.

— Don't criticize or argue with her or his experience. (You shouldn't feel that way! or What a dumb thing to think!)

— Sit so that you can see your partner's face when you are talking together.

— Put down the newspaper or book you are reading. Turn off the television.

Empathy
(refer to pages 35-36)

Try to recall an experience when you really felt listened to, understood, and accepted for who you are. Tell your partner what this was like for you.

Try to think of a time when you had difficulty understanding what was going on with your partner. See if you can explore what might help you get into his or her shoes. Sometimes it helps a lot to try imagining what is was like to grow up in your partner's family culture because it makes clearer why certain values are important to him or her.

_____

_____

_____

_____

_____

_____

Power — The Gift Of Collaboration, The Burden Of Hoarding

(refer to pages 46-47)

Take some time to think about your family of origin, your decision-making process, and your expectations for how you and your spouse-to-be will work out the details of your life together.

How were decisions made in your family? Did your parents make the decisions about family matters on their own? Were the children involved in discussions about family matters like moving, vacations, how they would be disciplined, whether they would get an allowance, etc.? Did you have "family conferences" where important topics were discussed? Did Mom and Dad make decisions for you (and your siblings)?

_____

_____

_____

_____

_____

_____

_____

Was one parent the final authority figure for the family? Did your parents divide decision-making on the basis of traditional gender roles? (i.e., Did your father take care of the finances and your mother take care of day-to-day decisions?)

_____

_____

_____

_____

_____

_____

_____

Did you see your parents disagree? Do you know how your parents worked out differences of opinion? Did one parent defer to the other when there was disagreement? Was it always the same parent, or did it depend on the issue?

_____

_____

_____

_____

_____

_____

What kinds of decisions were you allowed to make for yourself? Were you allowed to spend your money the way you wanted to? Choose your own career or college? Were you given the power and freedom to buy your own clothes or pick the extracurricular activities you wanted to do?

_____

_____

_____

_____

_____

_____

What did you do when you disagreed with your parents about something? Were you given the opportunity to talk it out? Did your parents have the final say?

_____

_____

_____

_____

_____

_____

How do you make decisions now? How do you and your spouse-to-be make decisions together? Does one of you make decisions about certain things, for example, what you do in your time together or what kind of wedding you'll have? What happens when you disagree about something? Does one of you defer to the other? Is one of you more likely than the other to want to talk things out? Does it depend on the issue?

_____

_____

_____

_____

_____

_____

Conflict
(refer to pages 47-51)

As an introduction to the collaborative process, take some time to work on the following conflict resolution exercise.

1.   Select one or two conflicts the two of you have had in the past.

2.   Try to determine whether this is a misunderstanding or a disagreement.

   Misunderstanding: "I thought you meant this, but discovered as we talked that you meant that" or "I just assumed when I heard you talking on the phone that you intended to ... but as we talked I realized that I had taken what you said out of context" or "When I saw you frowning at me, I thought you were angry with me and didn't know, until you told me later, that you had a headache."

   Disagreement: "I want to invite my mother to Thanksgiving dinner with us and you want us to eat alone" or "I want to relax after dinner with a newspaper and clean up later and you want to get the dishes done, the food put away as soon as we're done eating" (in other words, you understand each other very well, but disagree about an issue or area).

3. If your conflict was in fact a disagreement, at what step in the process toward negotiation and reconciliation did you stumble or get blocked?

4. Identify the issues of disagreement.

5. Decide on a time to discuss these.

6. Take turns hearing each person's perspective. What does each person want? Why?

7. Check that each has accurately heard the other's perspective.

8. Brainstorm about alternatives. (This is a time for creativity!)

9. Consider prayerfully what the two of you are discussing.

10. Make a decision and plans for future review and evaluation of your joint decision.

Power And Anger
(refer to page 54)

Anger Exercise: Take a few moments to answer the following questions. See how you deal with/react to anger and then talk about your answers with your partner.

1. What words or pictures come to mind when you try to describe anger?

2. How did your parents express their anger toward you and toward each other?

3. What conflict management styles did they tend to use? Avoiding, competing, accommodating, compromising, collaborating?

4. How did other members of your family deal with anger and conflict?

5. Describe what your feelings were when someone was angry with you.

6. How did your family react when you got angry?

7. How do you react when your partner is angry?

8. Do you respond any differently when s/he is angry with you?

9. How do you let your partner know that you are angry?

10. How do you let her/him know that you are "over" your anger?

11. Are there other feelings you associate with being angry?

12. How would you describe yourself? As slow or quick to anger? As one who holds a grudge or is quick to forgive and forget?

These questions are adapted from *Couples in Treatment: Techniques and Approaches for Effective Practice*, Gerald R. Weeks and Stephen Treat, Brunner/ Mazel, 1992.

Security — The Gift Of Commitment, The Burden Of Anxiety

(refer to pages 59-62)

SECURITY

Anxiety - - - - - - - - Relative Absence of Threat - - - - - - - - Anxiety
Fear of chaos   Fear of abandonment
Response is creating   Response is dependence on
good order   partner or security "stuff"

Using the continuum above and illustration on page 58 of the handbook to notice some of your ideas about security and your anxieties, read the questions below, jot down some notes about your observations, and then share your thinking with your partner. Perhaps as you talk together, you will better understand and cope with the expressions of security and anxiety in your relationship.

What did you learn about security in your family culture? (You can get at this question, too, by thinking about your family's biggest worry.)

_____

_____

_____

_____

_____

Do you see any connections between what you learned there and your expectations of your partner?

_____

_____

_____

_____

_____

Were there any "events" in the life of your family similar to the death of Mark's mother or Melissa's aunt's divorce and move away? How did these affect you?

_____

_____

_____

_____

_____

_____

_____

How did you know when members of your family were worried? Did they tell you or did you notice certain changes in the way they behaved?

_____

_____

_____

_____

_____

_____

_____

What do you think you worry about most?

_____

_____

_____

_____

_____

_____

_____

What do you do about it to try to make yourself feel calmer and less anxious?

_____

_____

_____

_____

_____

_____

Is there something, someone, some activity you think might operate as your "security blanket"?

_____

_____

_____

_____

_____

_____

What do you think your partner worries most about?

_____

_____

_____

_____

_____

How do you know when she/he is anxious and worried?

_____

_____

_____

_____

_____

How do you try to make things safe again with each other?

_____

_____

_____

_____

_____

_____

Do you see any similarities between the two of you in the ways you manage anxiety? Do you see any differences?

_____

_____

_____

_____

_____

_____

Thinking about your responses to the questions above, identify at least two things you think might be key to maintaining trust and stability in your relationship.

_____

_____

_____

_____

_____

_____

Marital Comfort Zones

Reread the three scenarios on pages 63-65 of the handbook, each one describing a common relationship situation in which individual comfort zones are jostled. See if you find yourself identifying with any of these situations, then share your reactions with your partner.

Freedom/Responsibility —
The Gift Of Responsible Choice,
The Burden Of Self-preoccupation

You Are Uniquely Made, Uniquely Gifted
(refer to pages 72-73)

Take time now to reflect about yourselves in terms of your uniqueness. Think about your families of origin, your personalities, your tastes, preferences, your attitudes and values about money, children, work, church, religion, recreation, friendship, your ways of showing affection, appreciation, anger, etc.

What similarities do you notice between you?

_____
_____
_____
_____
_____
_____
_____
_____

In what ways do you think these similarities are good for your relationship? Are there ways in which these are not so good? Why?

_____
_____
_____
_____
_____
_____
_____
_____

What differences (differentness) do you notice between you?

_____

_____

_____

_____

_____

_____

_____

_____

In what ways do you think these are good for your relationship? Are there ways in which these are not so good? Why?

_____

_____

_____

_____

_____

_____

_____

_____

Can you see any places where these personal differences are two sides of the same coin?

_____

_____

_____

_____

_____

_____

_____

_____

Affirmation And Appreciation Of Each Other
(refer to pages 73-74)

Take some time now to think about your own relationship by completing the following sentences:

I feel appreciated as a unique person, loved, important, and valued by my partner when ...

_____

_____

_____

_____

_____

_____

_____

I feel less appreciated or even taken for granted and unimportant when my partner ...

_____

_____

_____

_____

_____

_____

_____

I show my partner I appreciate, love, and value him/her when ...

_____

_____

_____

_____

_____

_____

_____

The way I can tell that my partner feels unappreciated or unimportant is that he/she ...

_____

_____

_____

_____

_____

_____

I would like my spouse to do this more often (e.g., express his/her feelings about me/our relationship; affirm something I do; say "thank you," etc.) ...

_____

_____

_____

_____

_____

_____

I would like to show my partner I appreciate him/her more often by ...

_____

_____

_____

_____

_____

_____

Now take time to exchange and talk over your responses with each other.

CPSIA information can be obtained at www.ICGtesting.com
Printed in the USA
BVOW021225090212

282559BV00007B/12/P